GOLDEN RETRIEVER
COLORING BOOKS

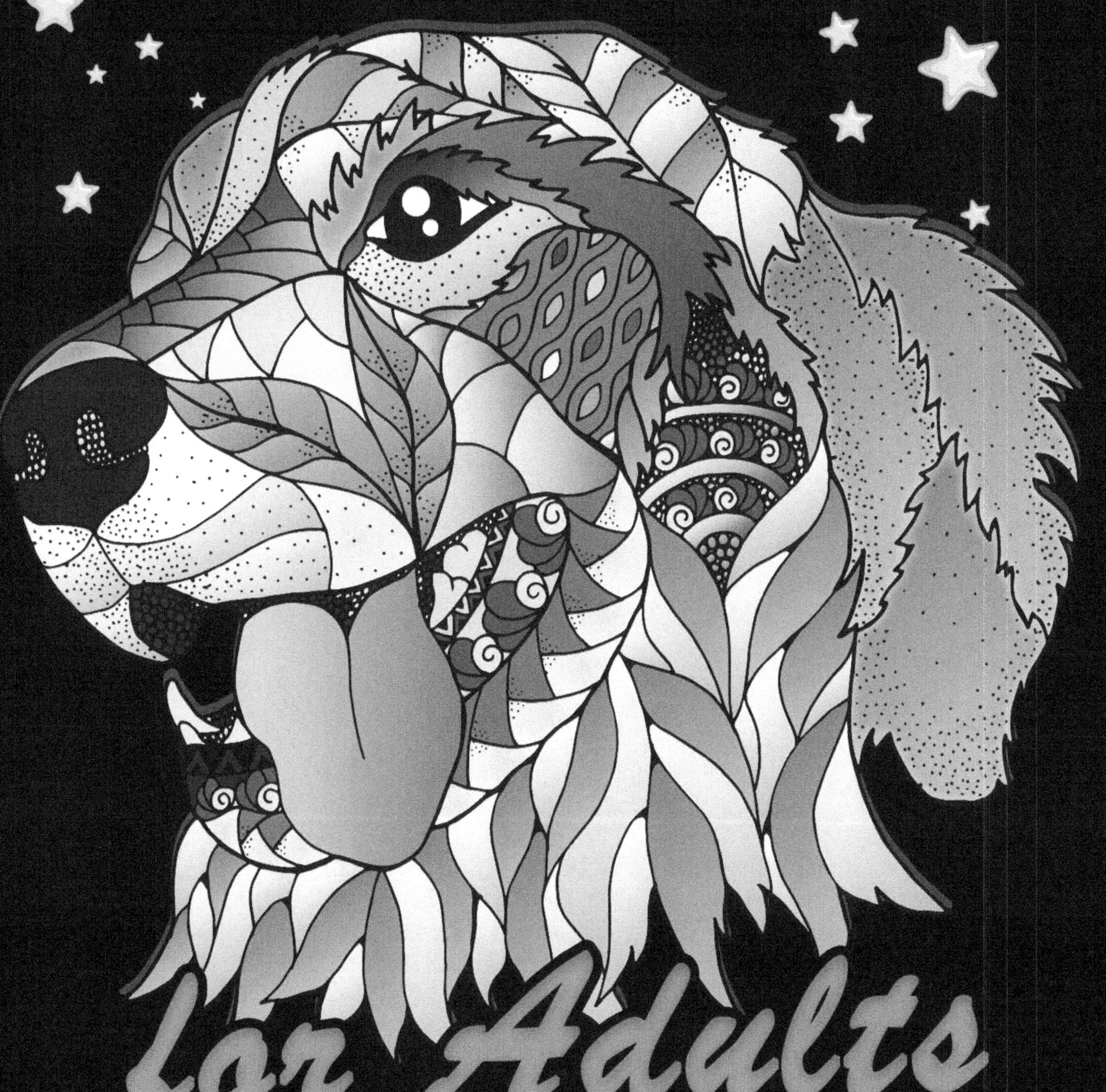

for Adults

PUBLISHED IN 2018 BY
KODOMO PUBLISHING

PRINTED IN THE UNITED STATES OF AMERICA

COLOR TEST PAGE

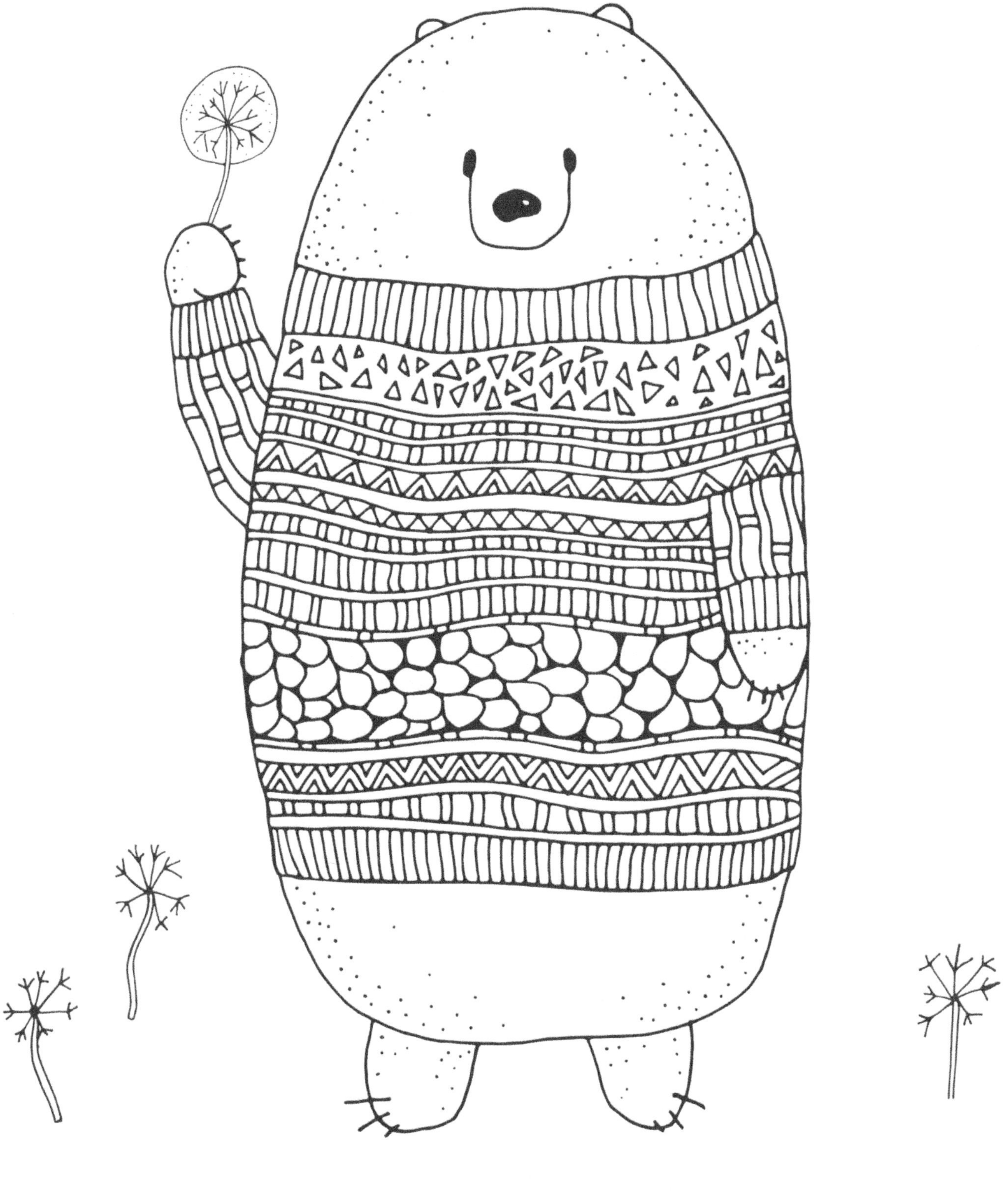

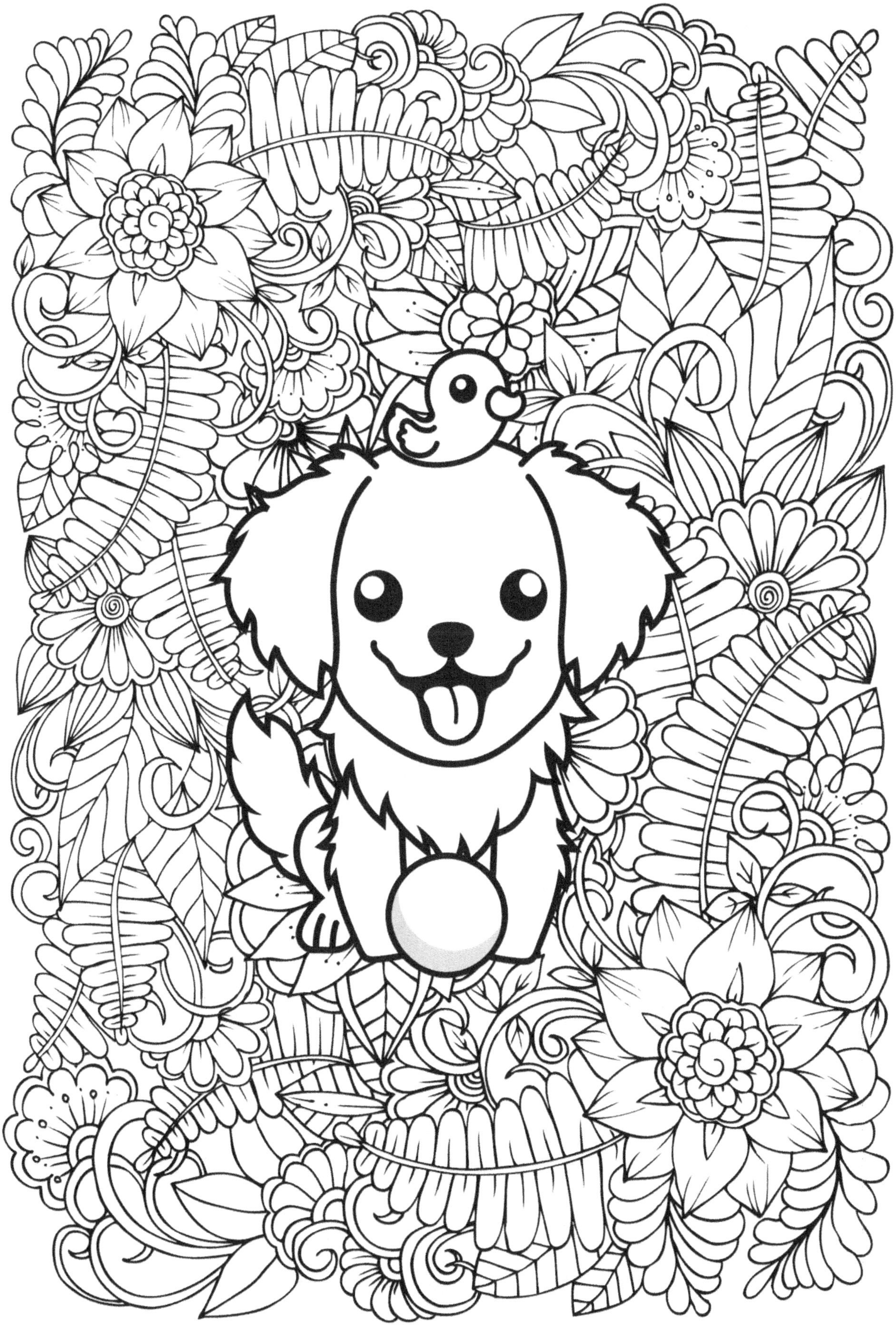

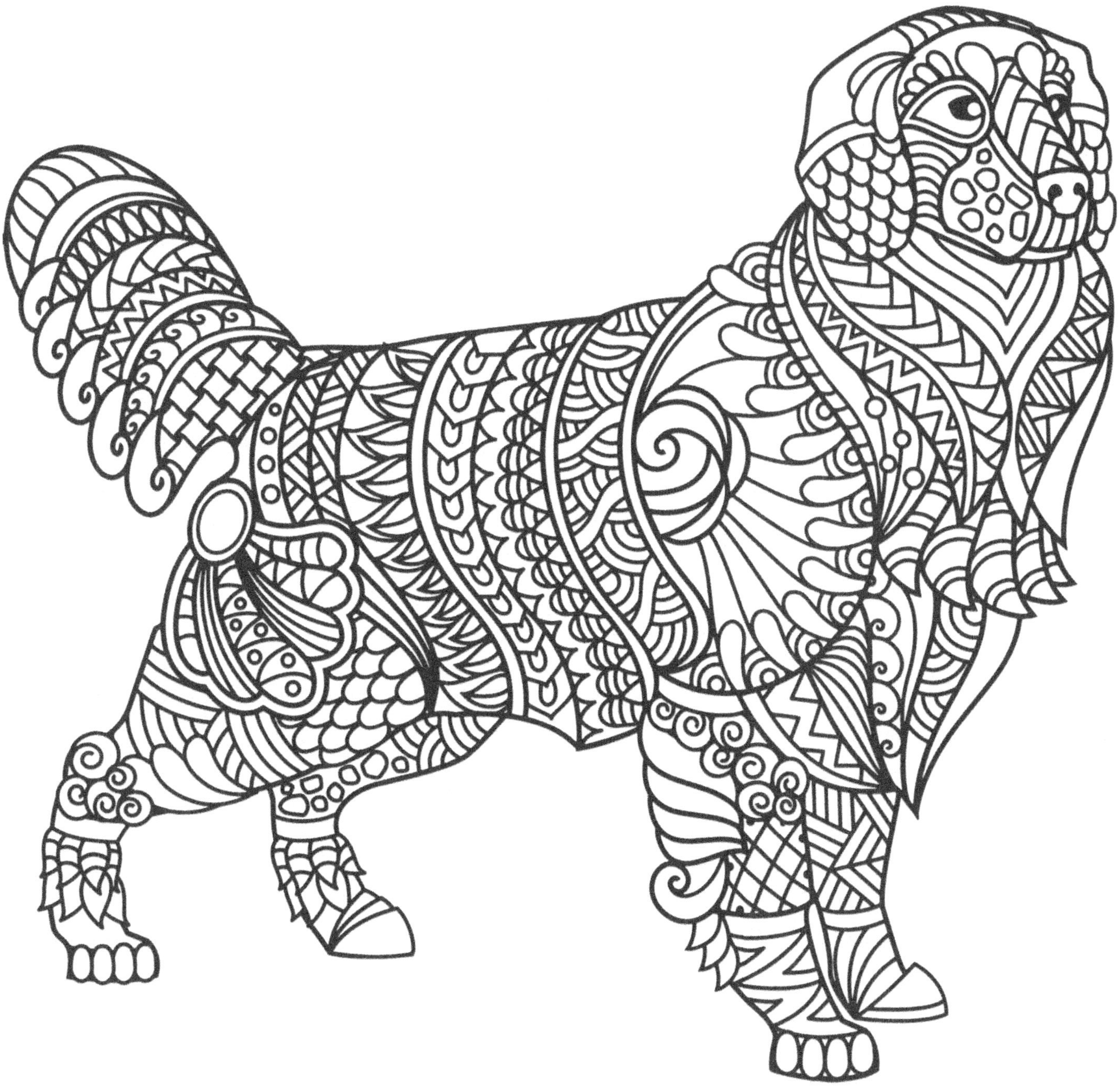

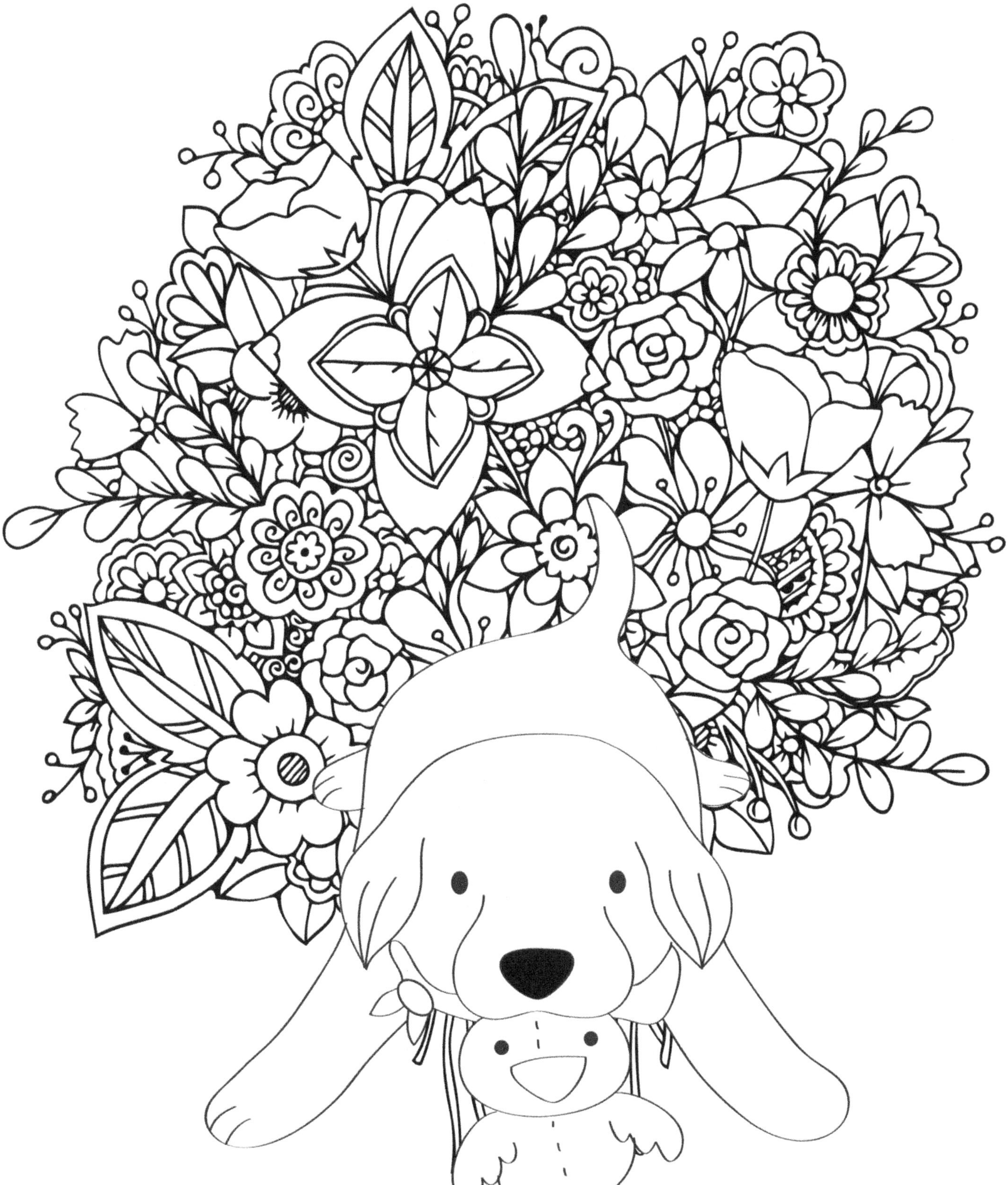

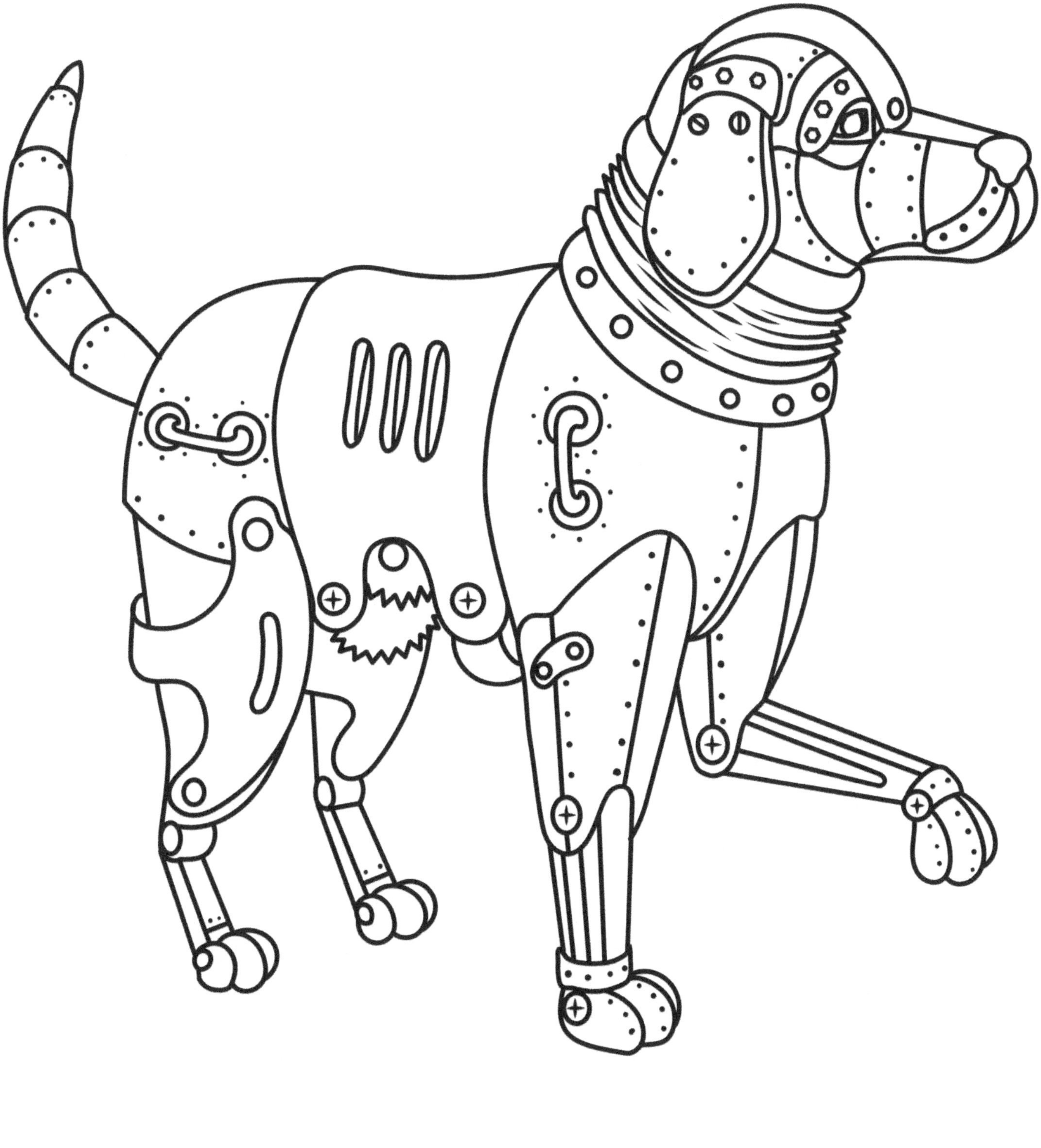

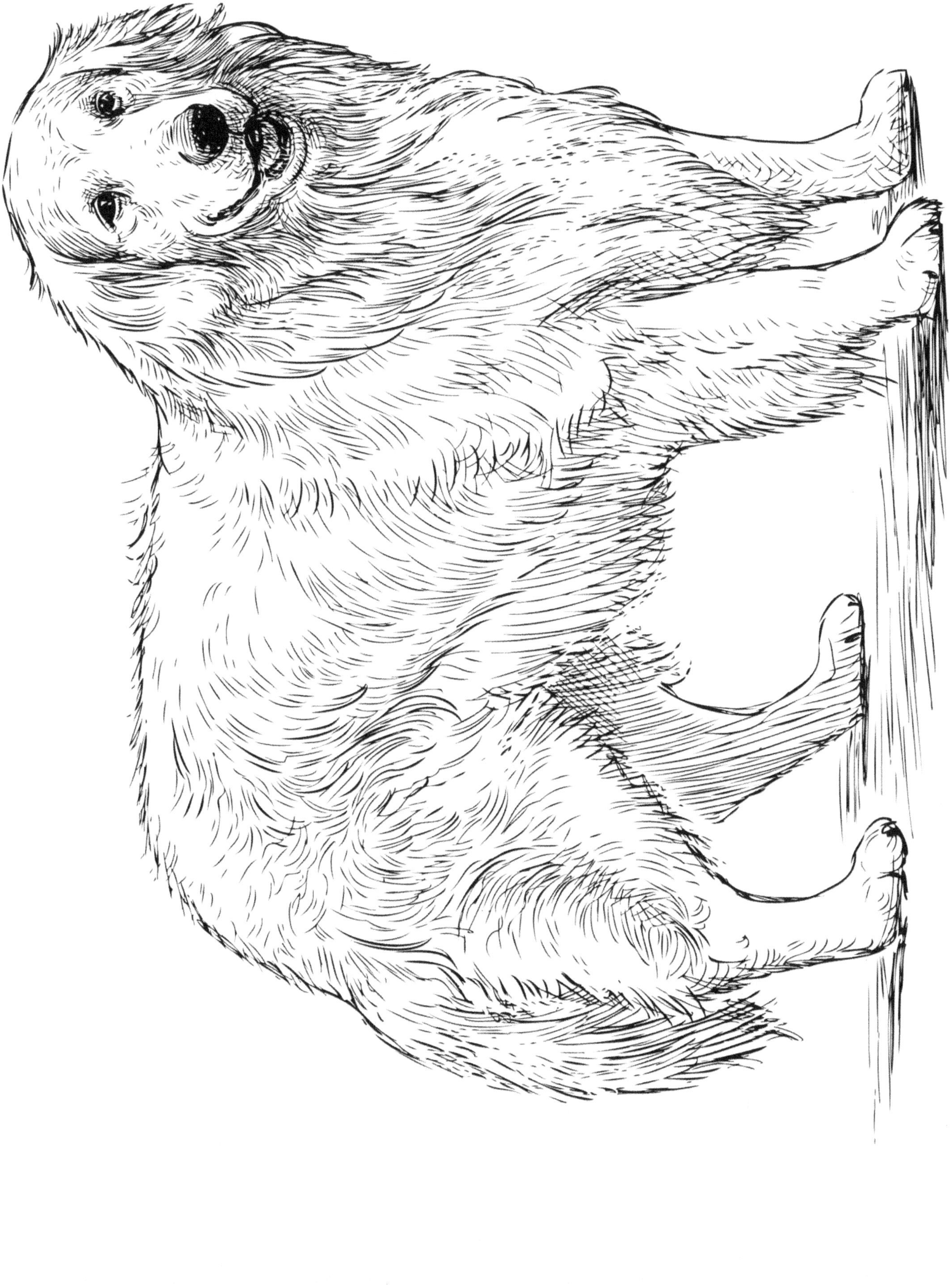

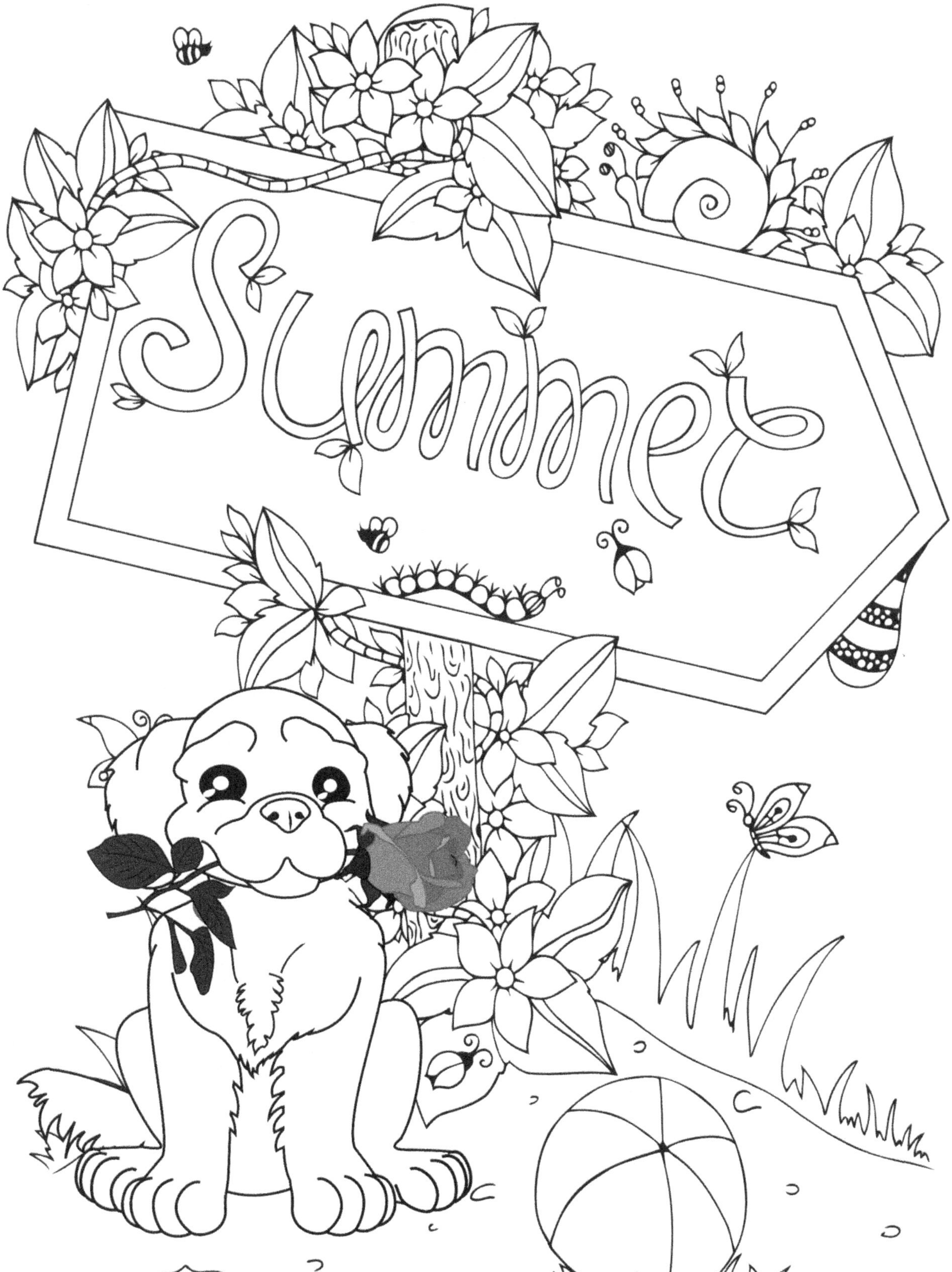
Summer

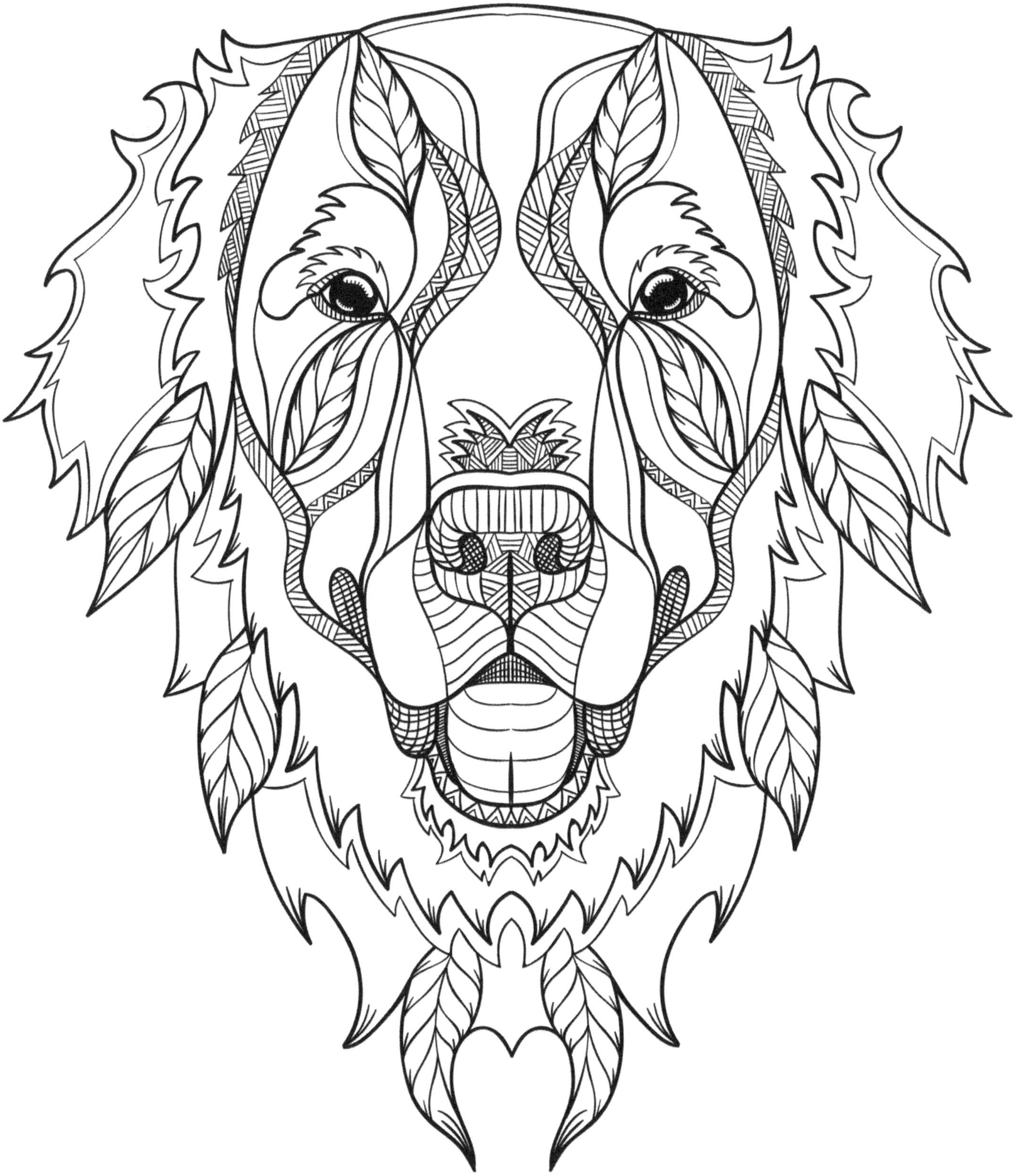

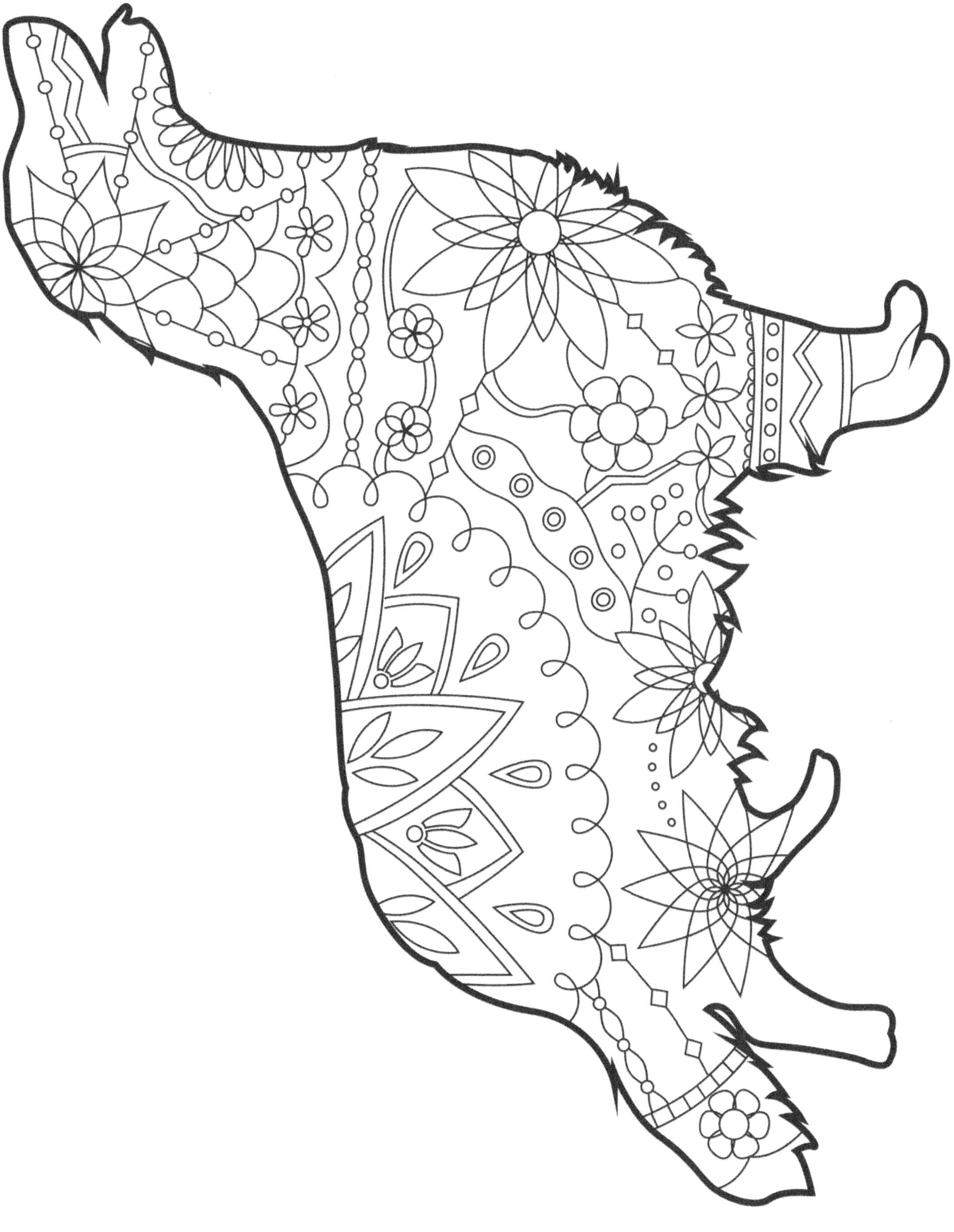

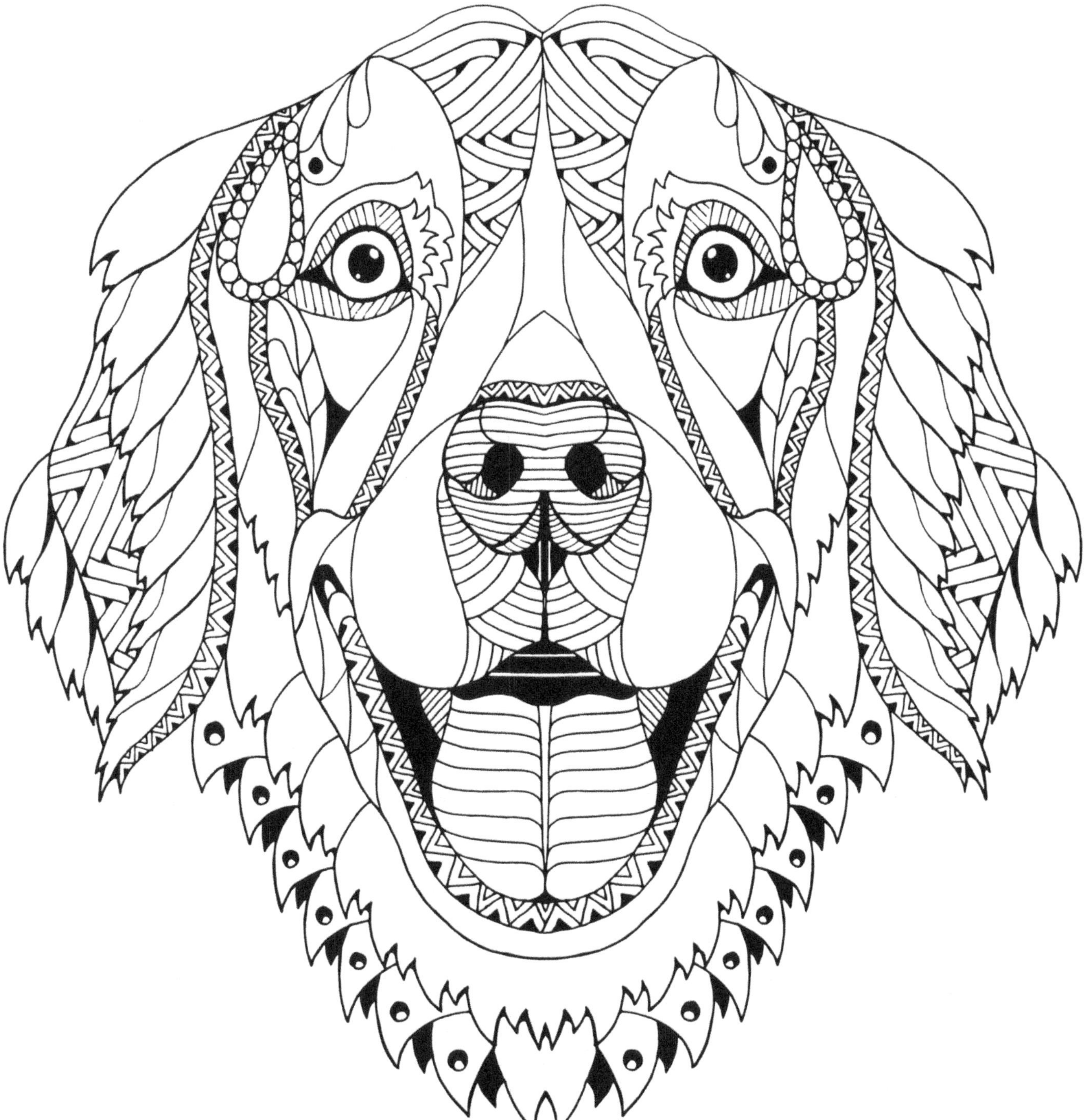

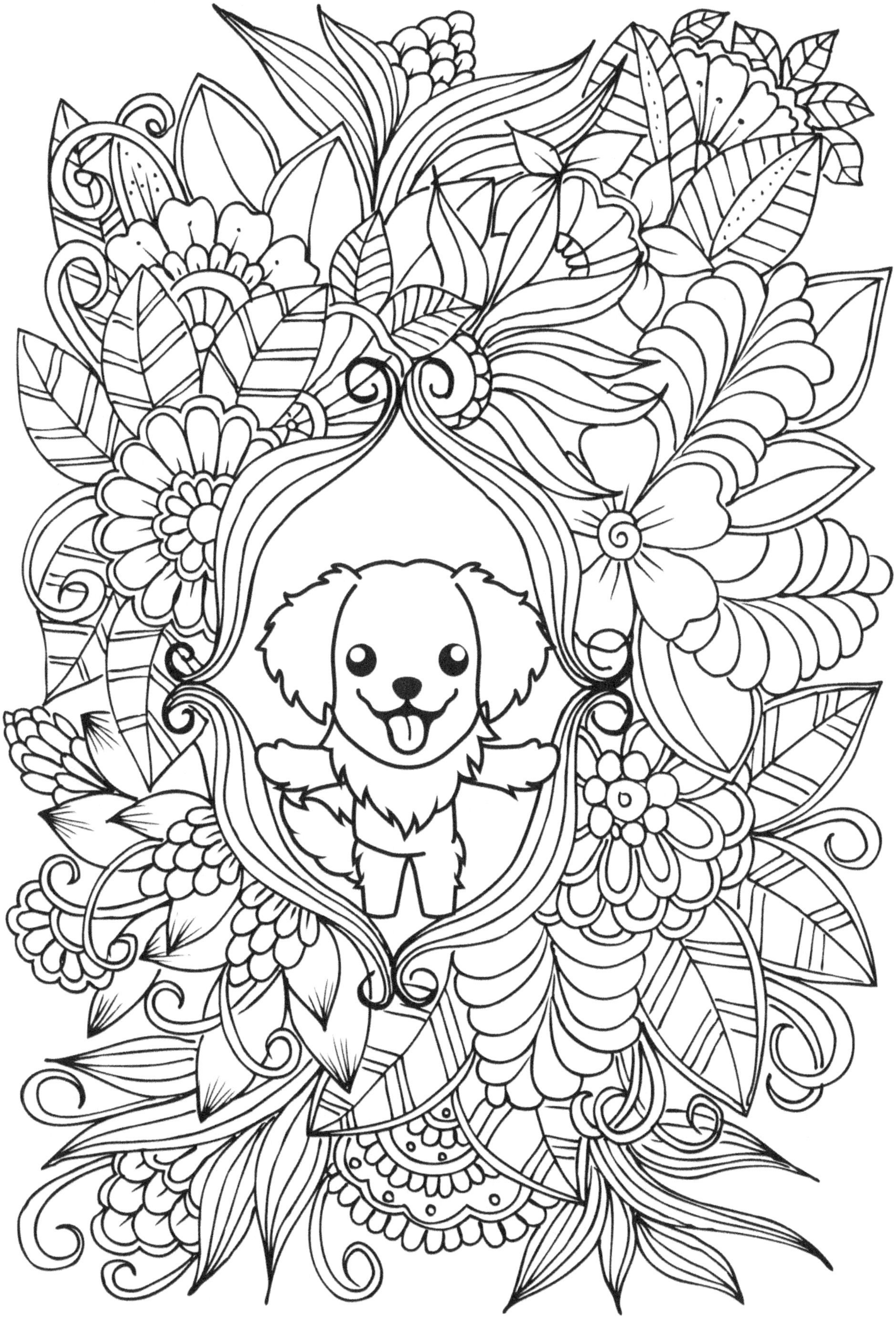

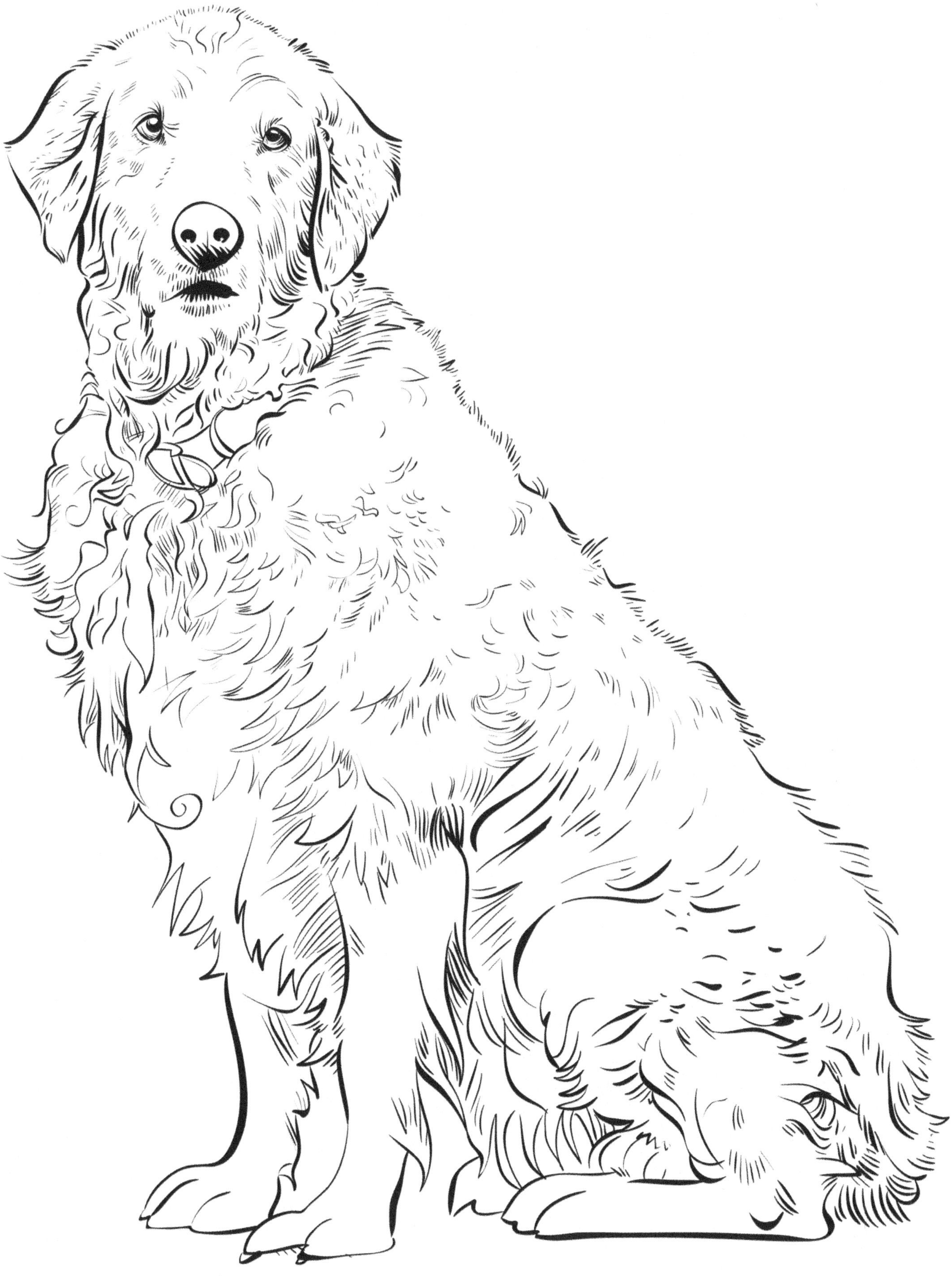

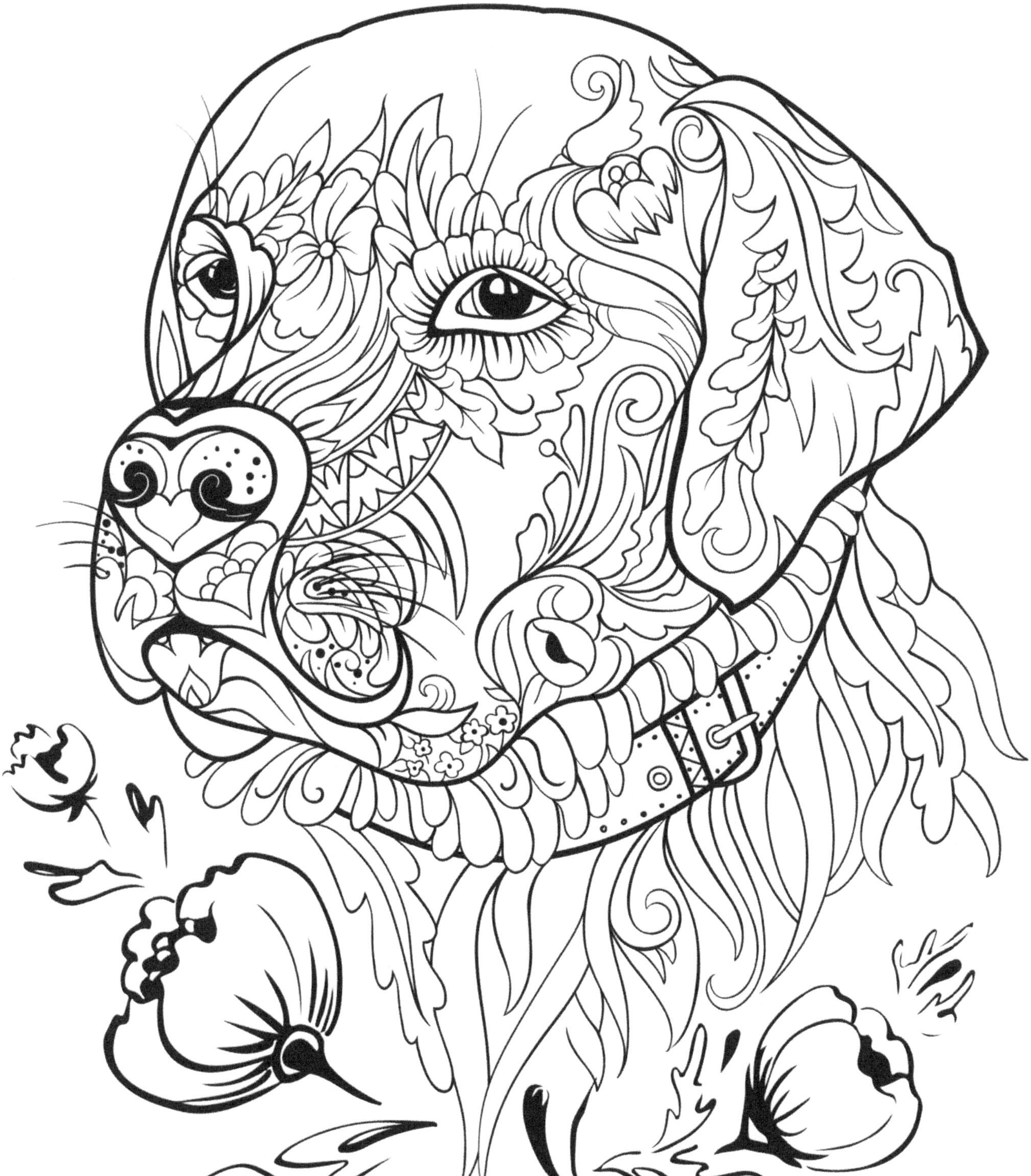

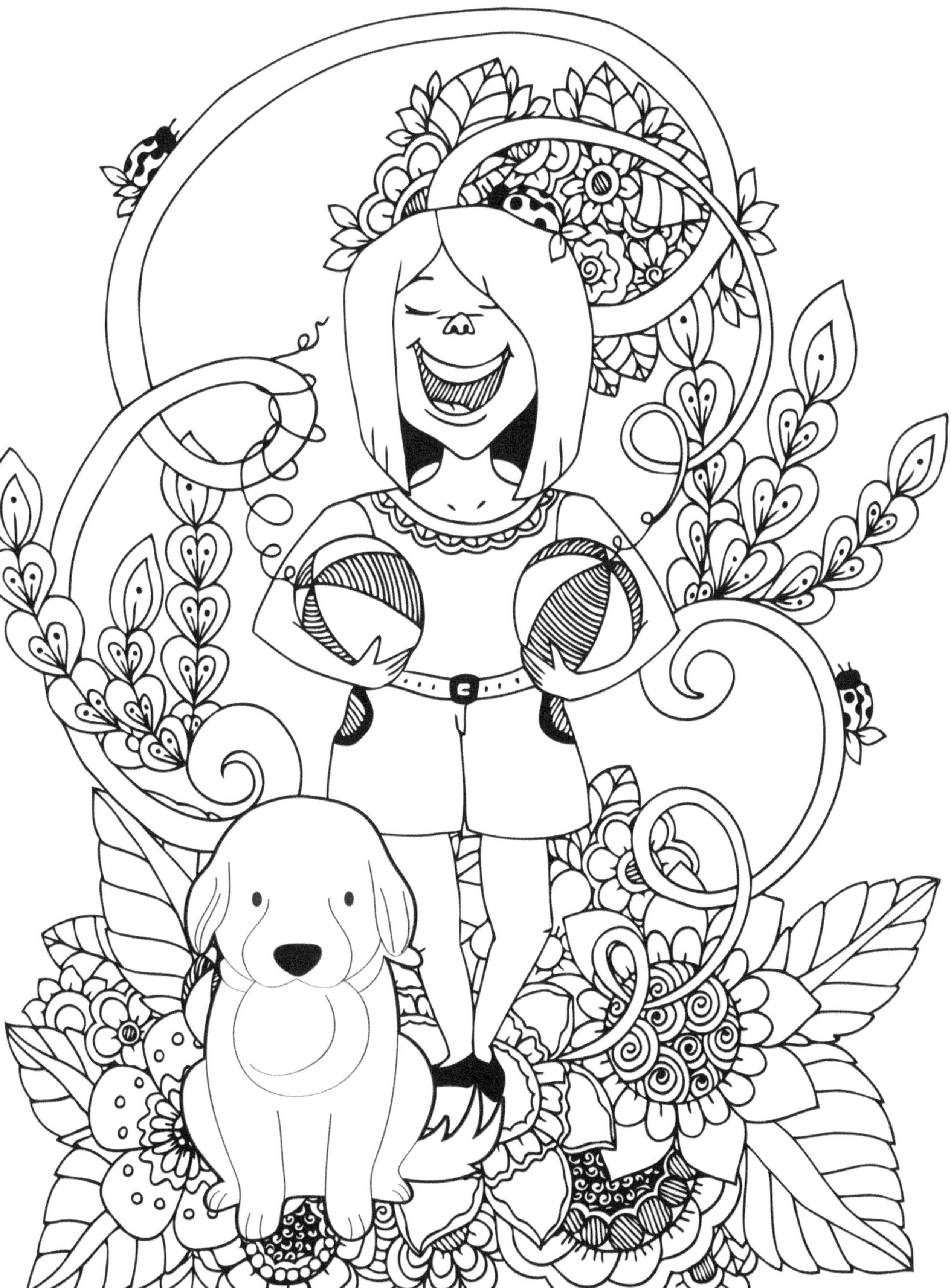

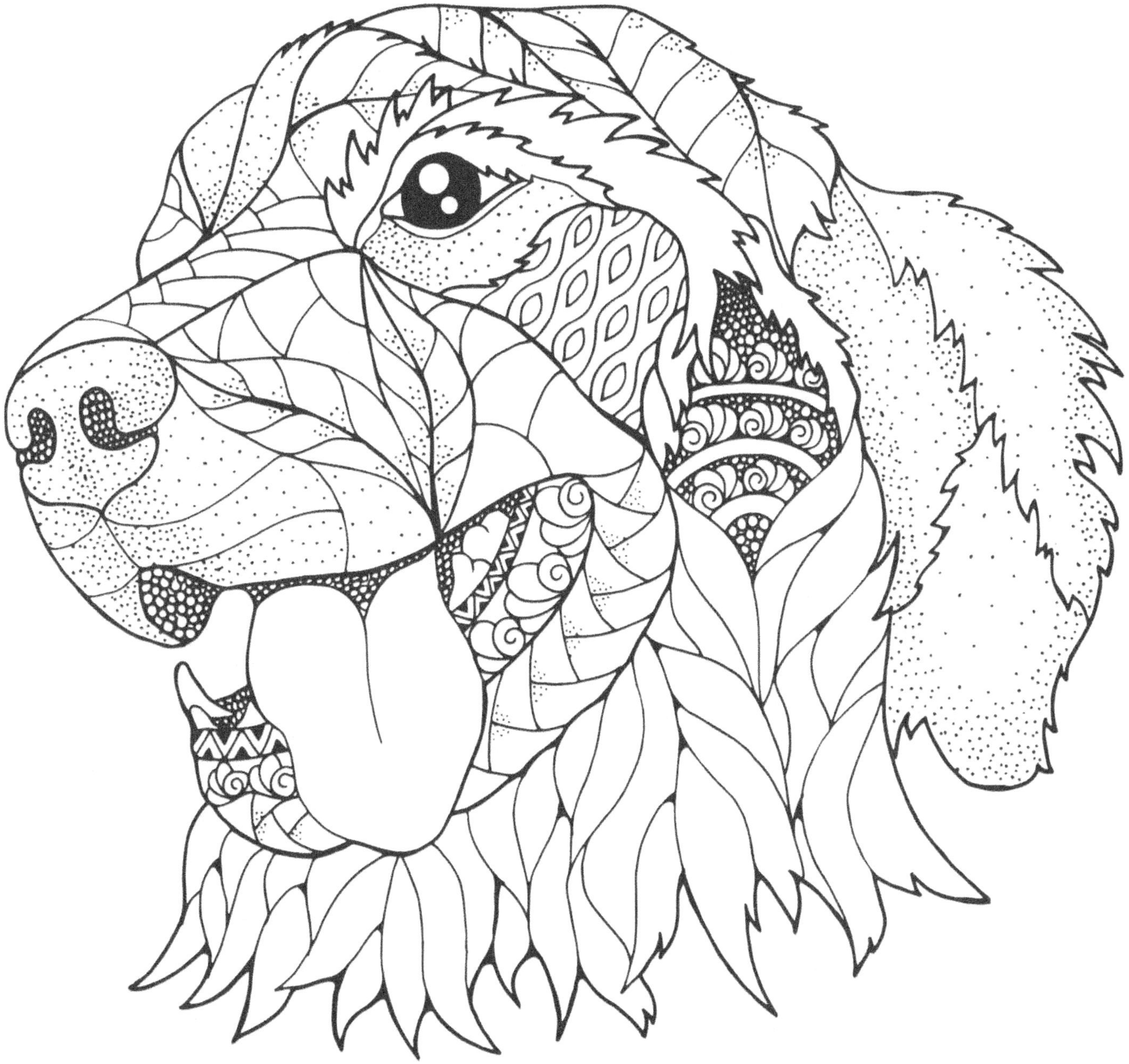

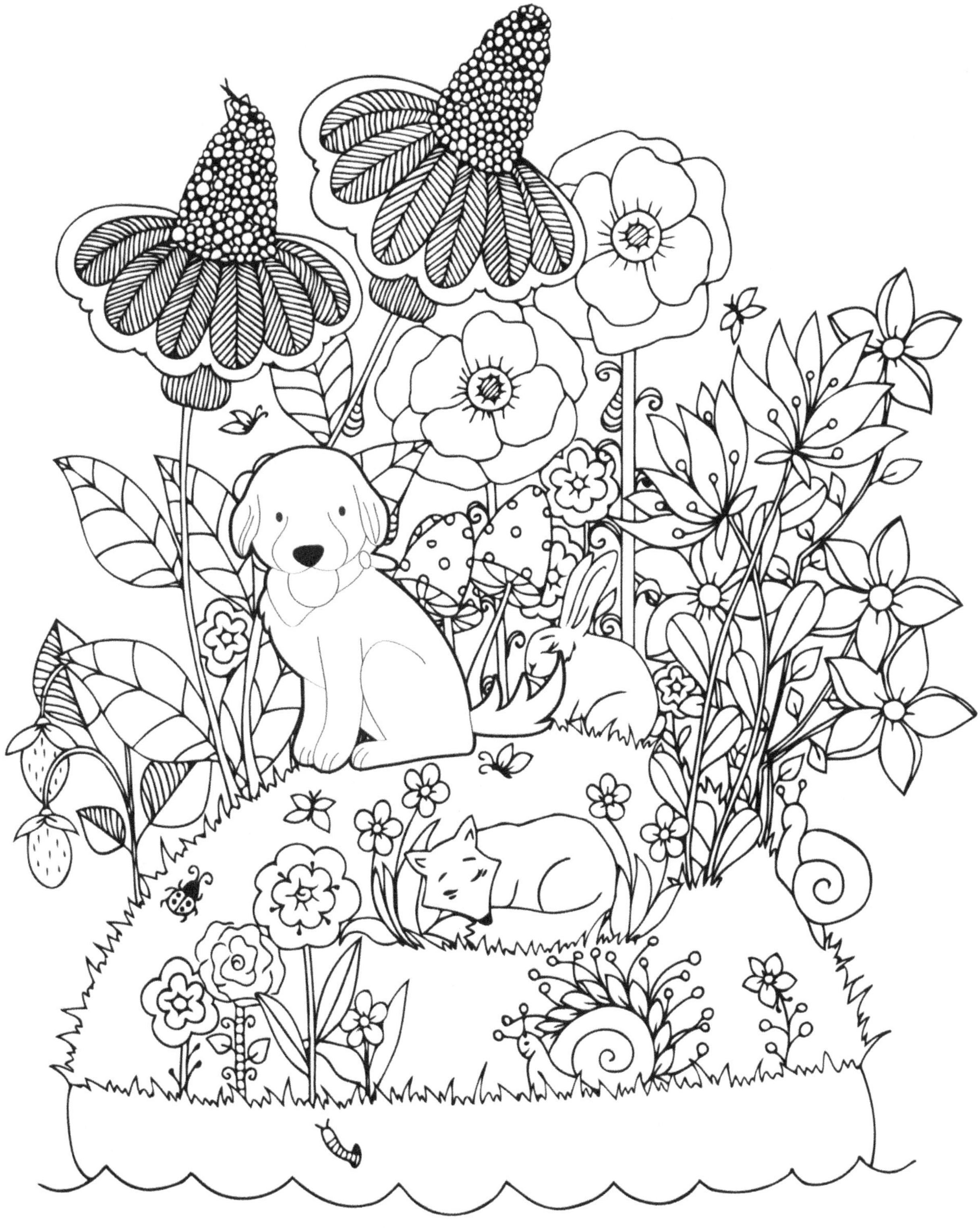

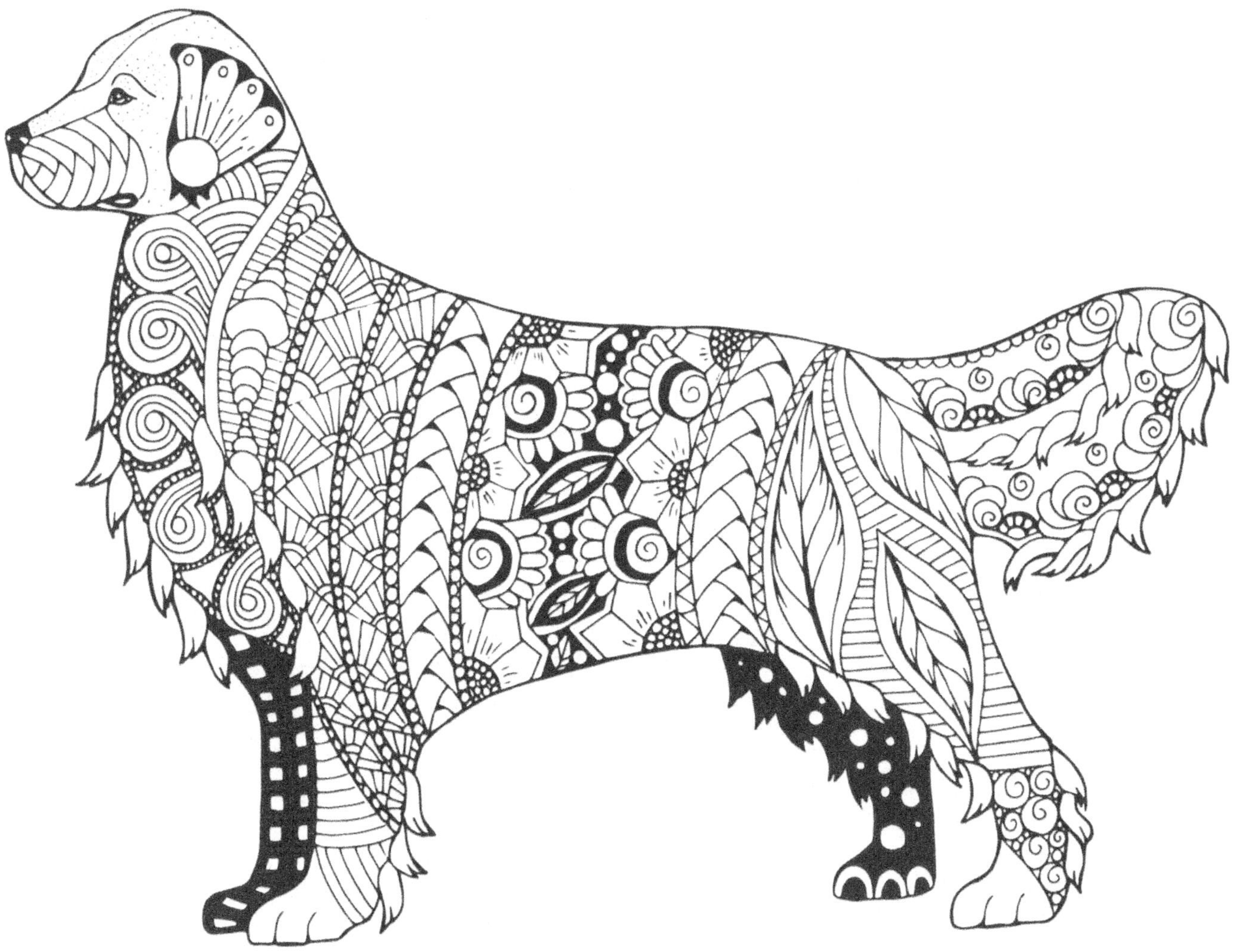

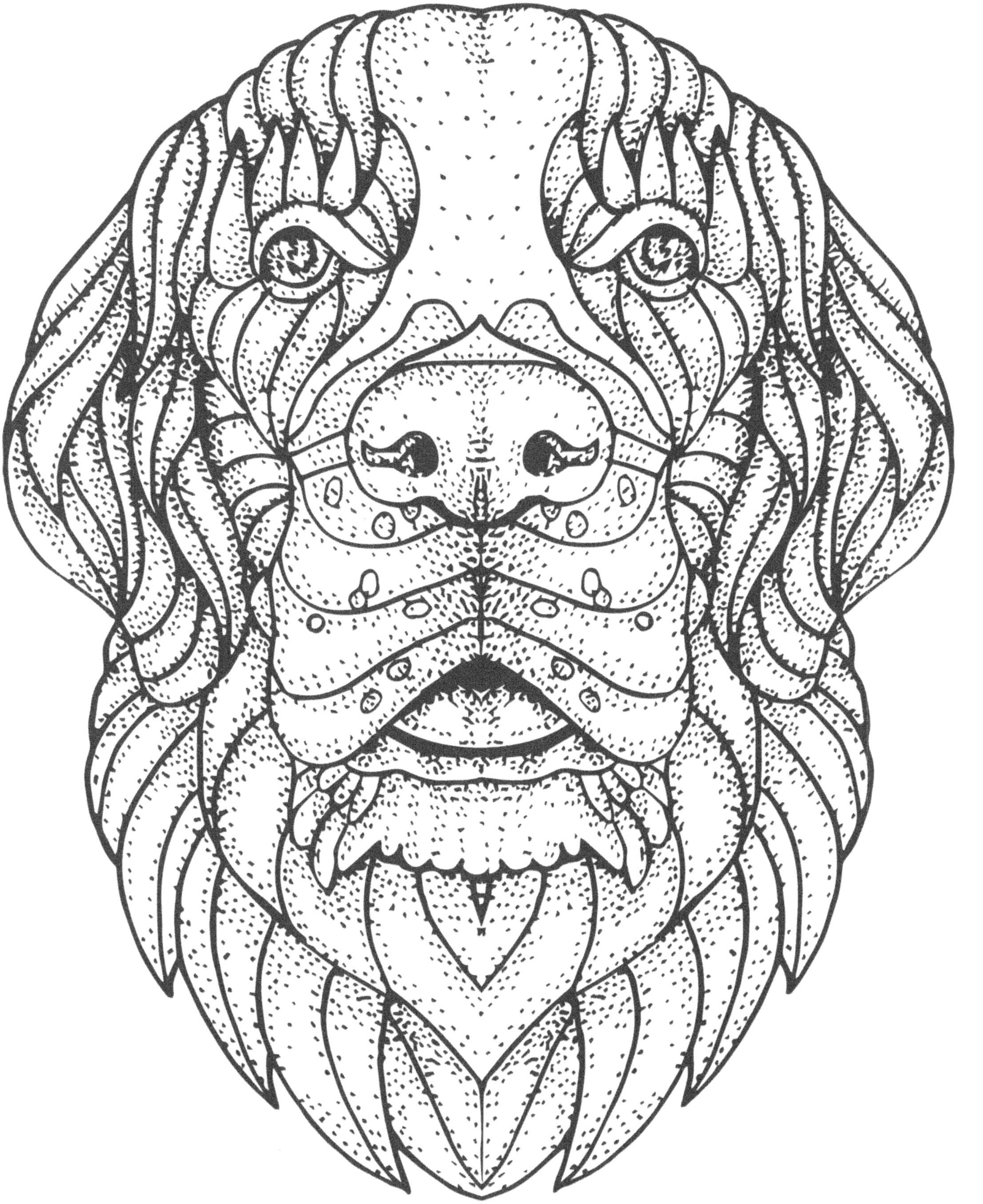

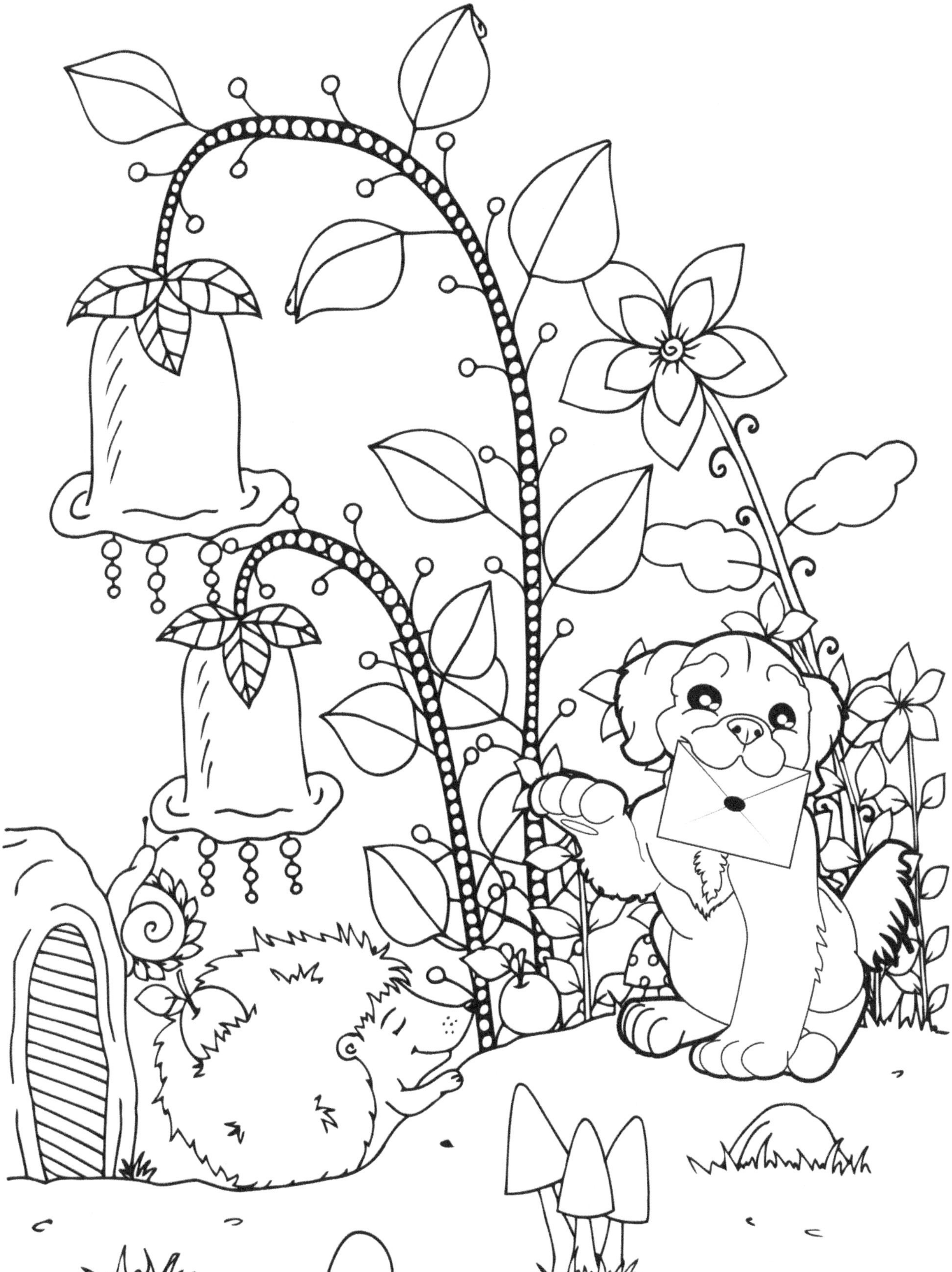

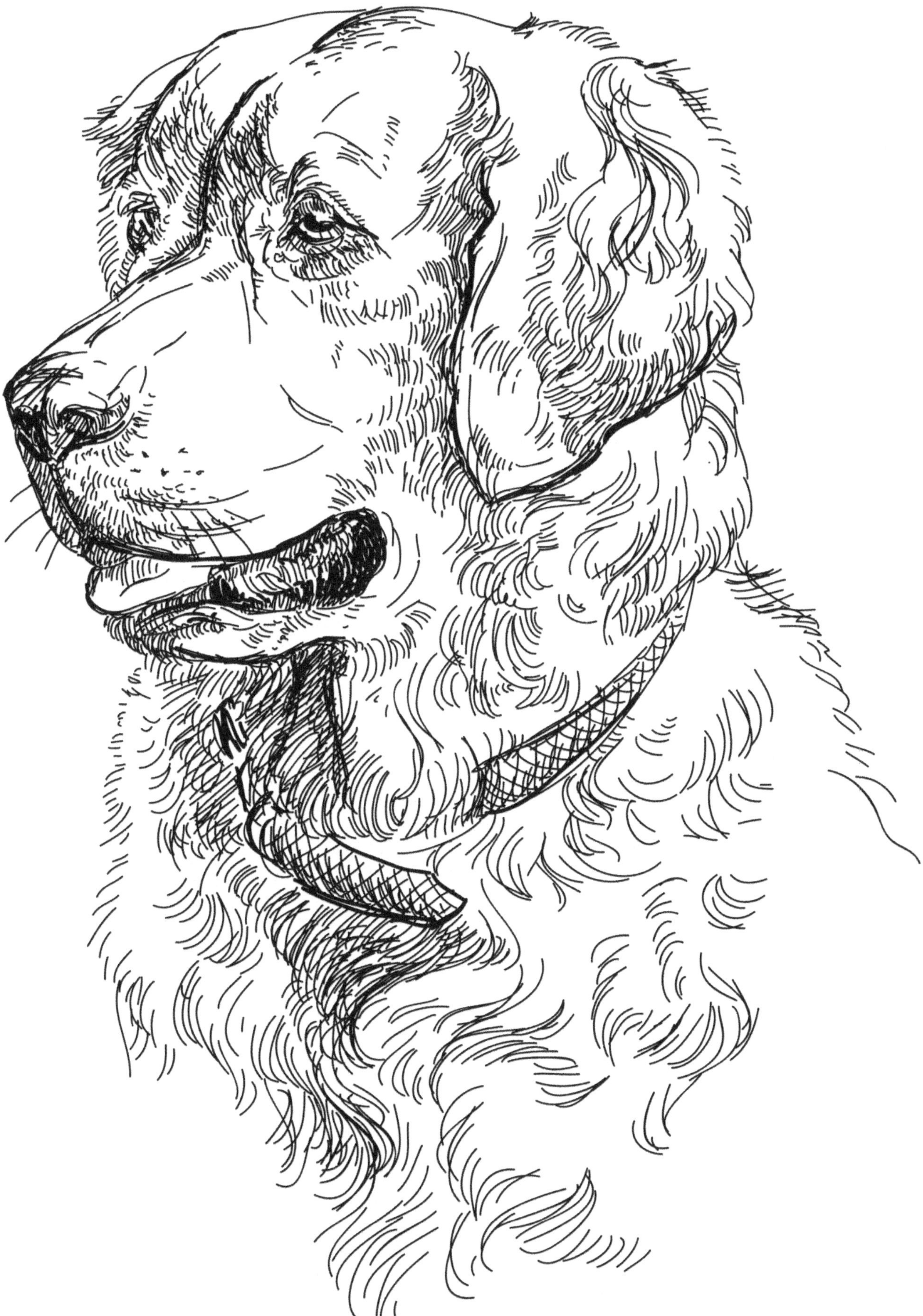

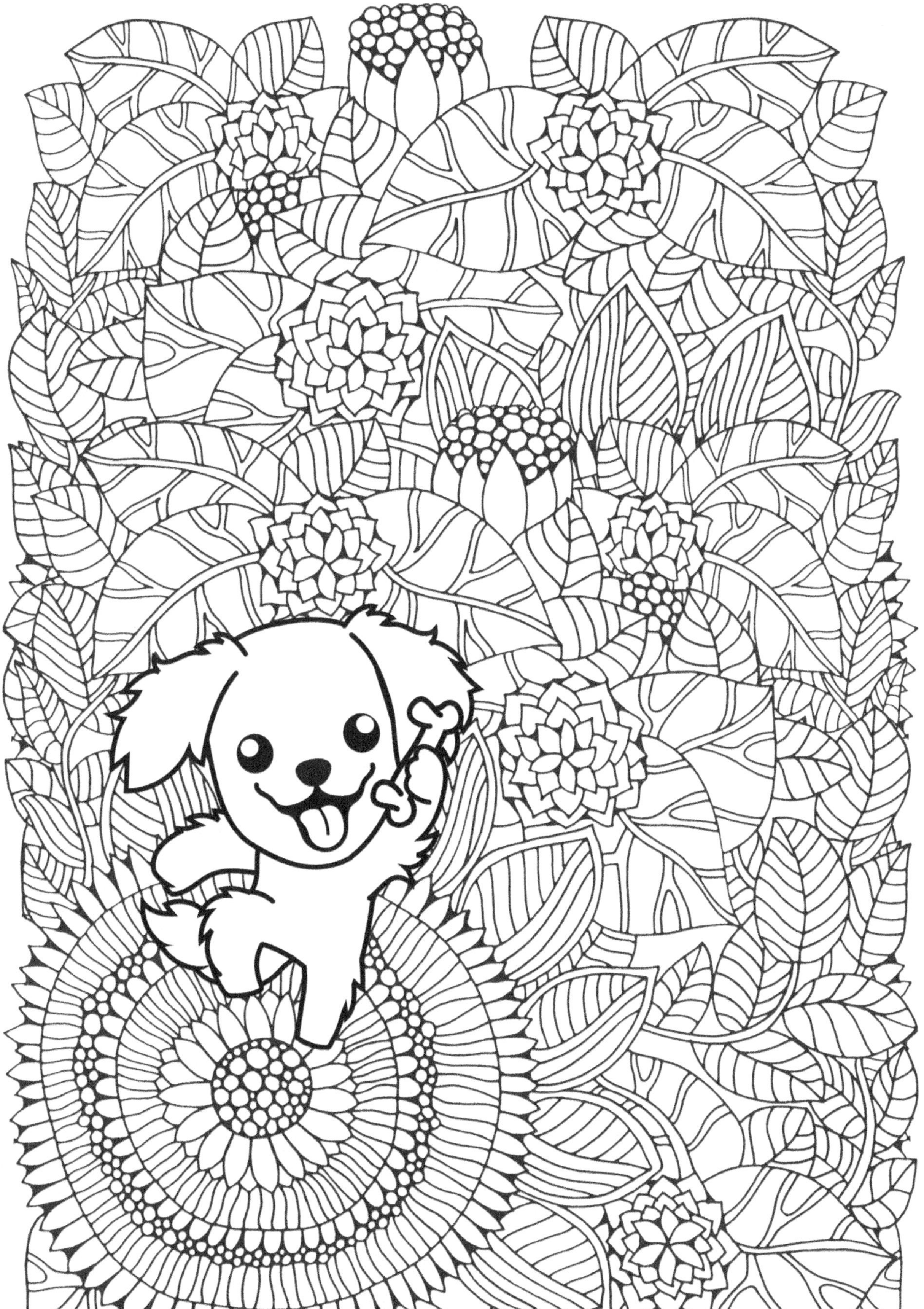

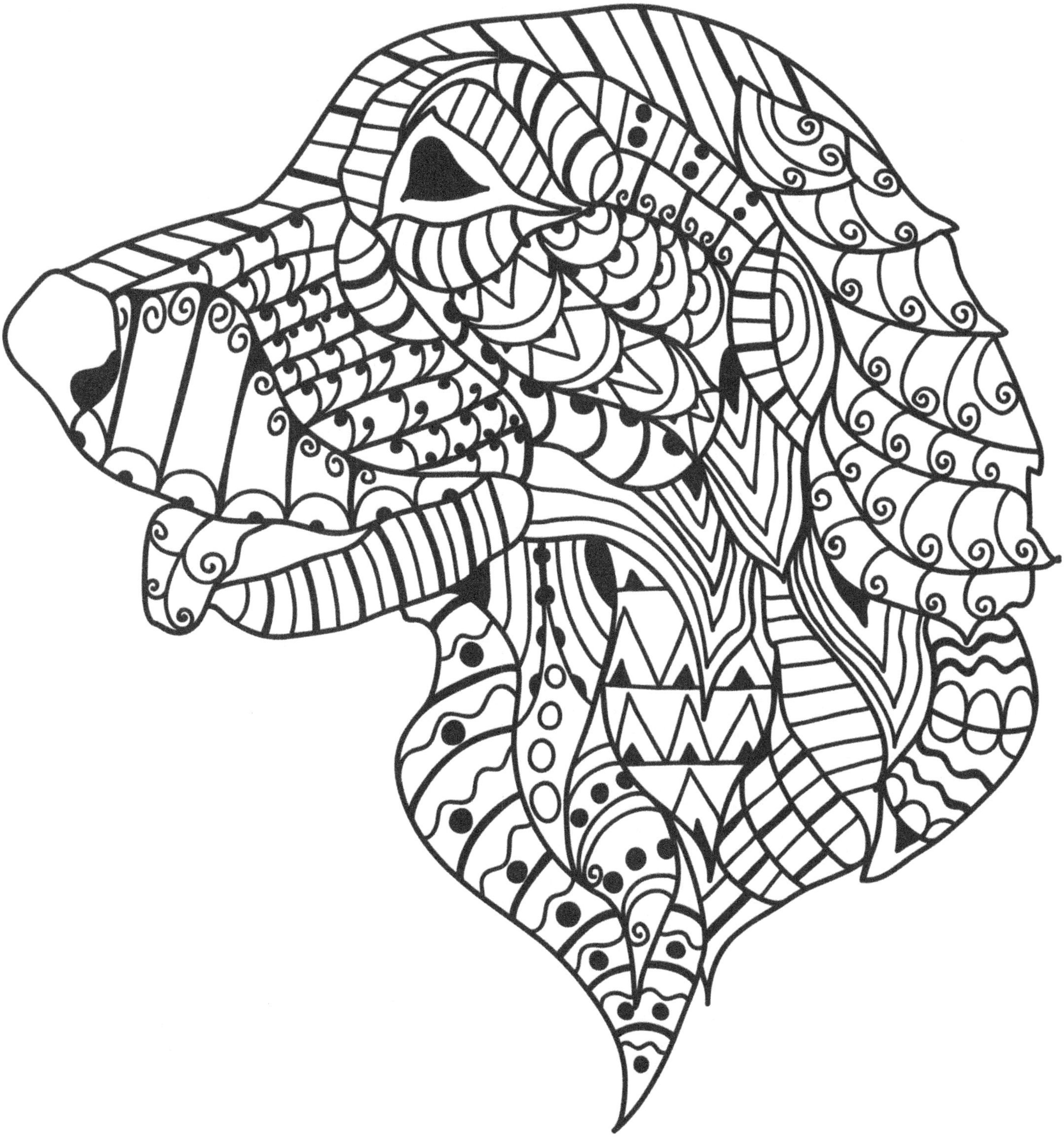

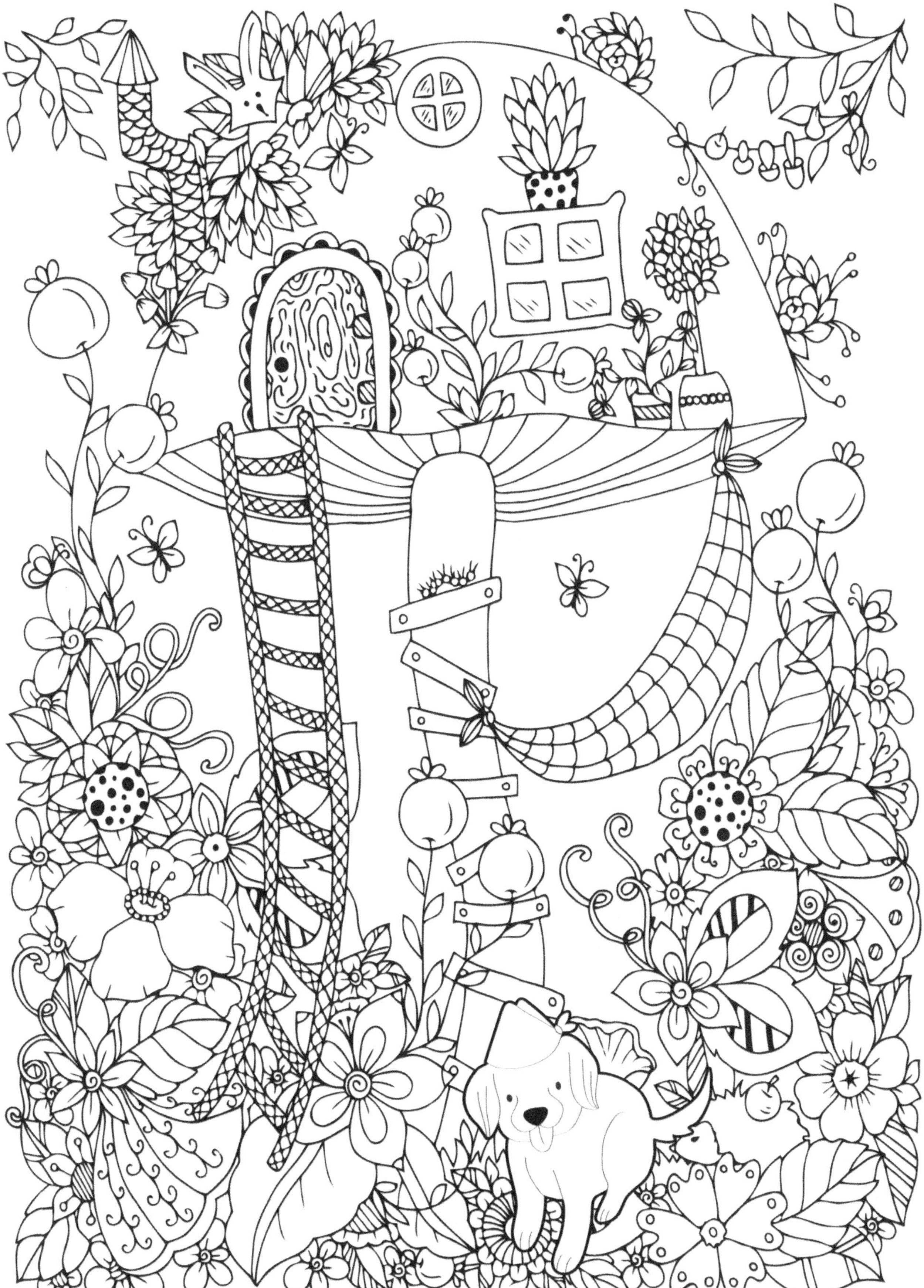

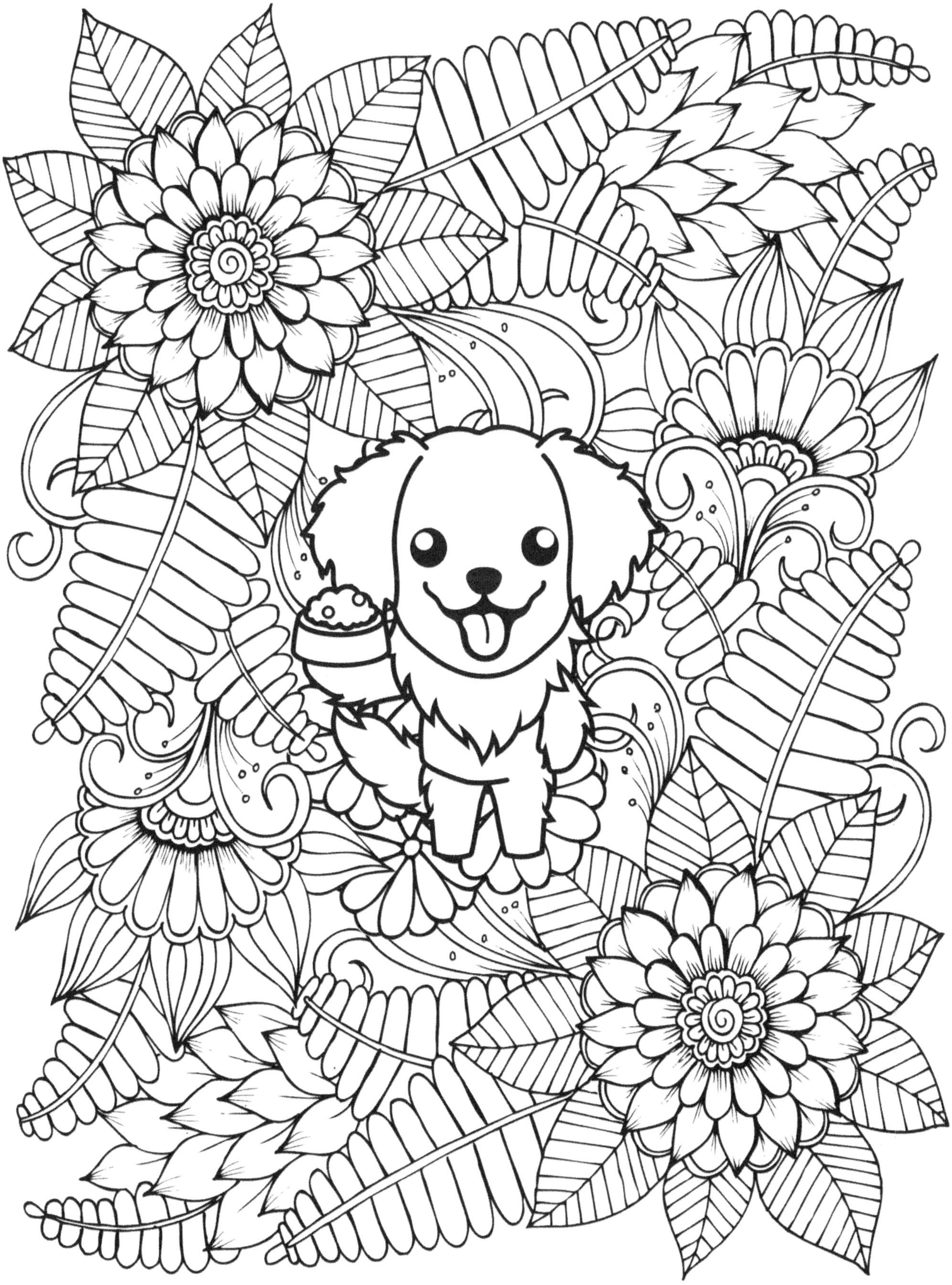

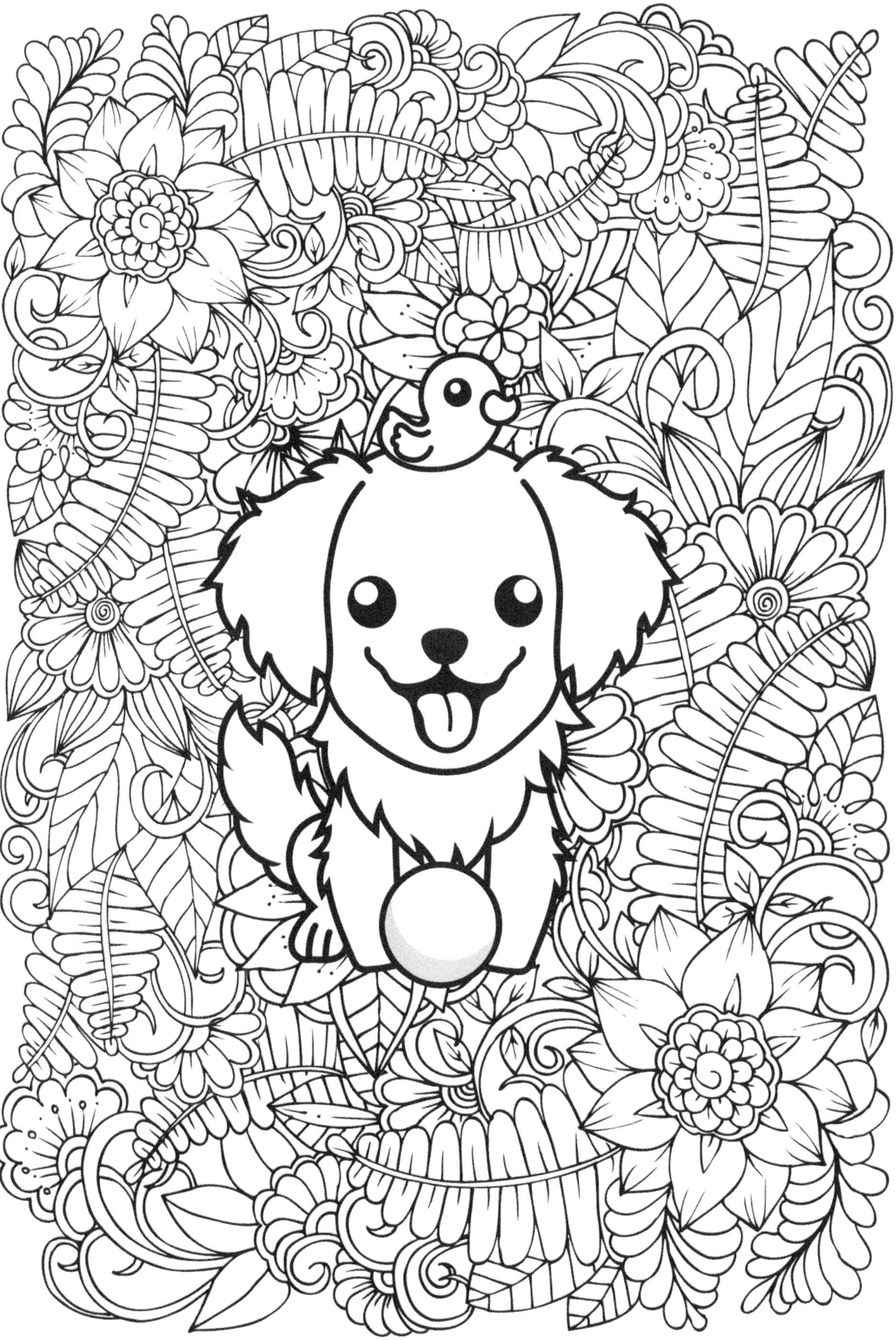

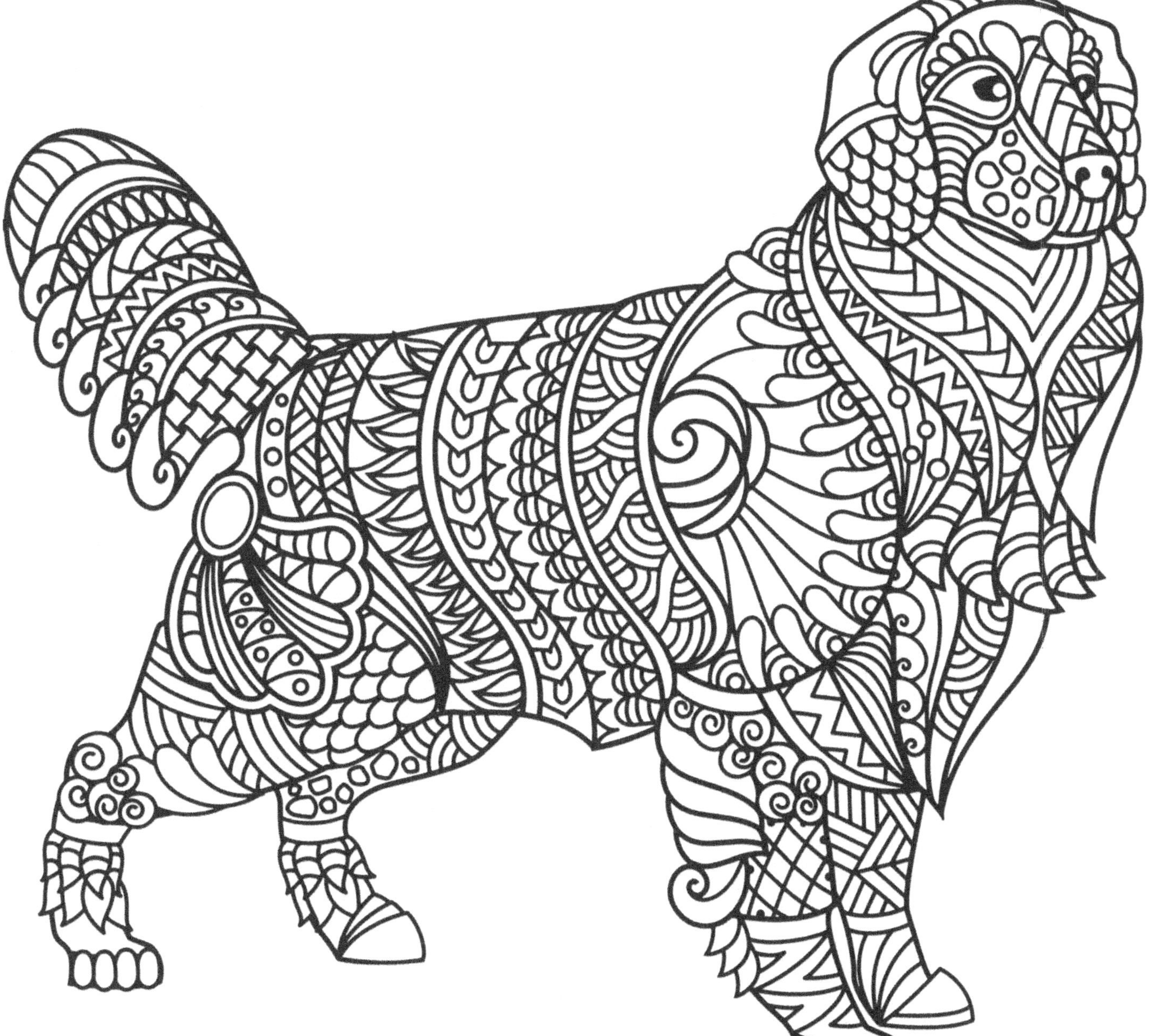

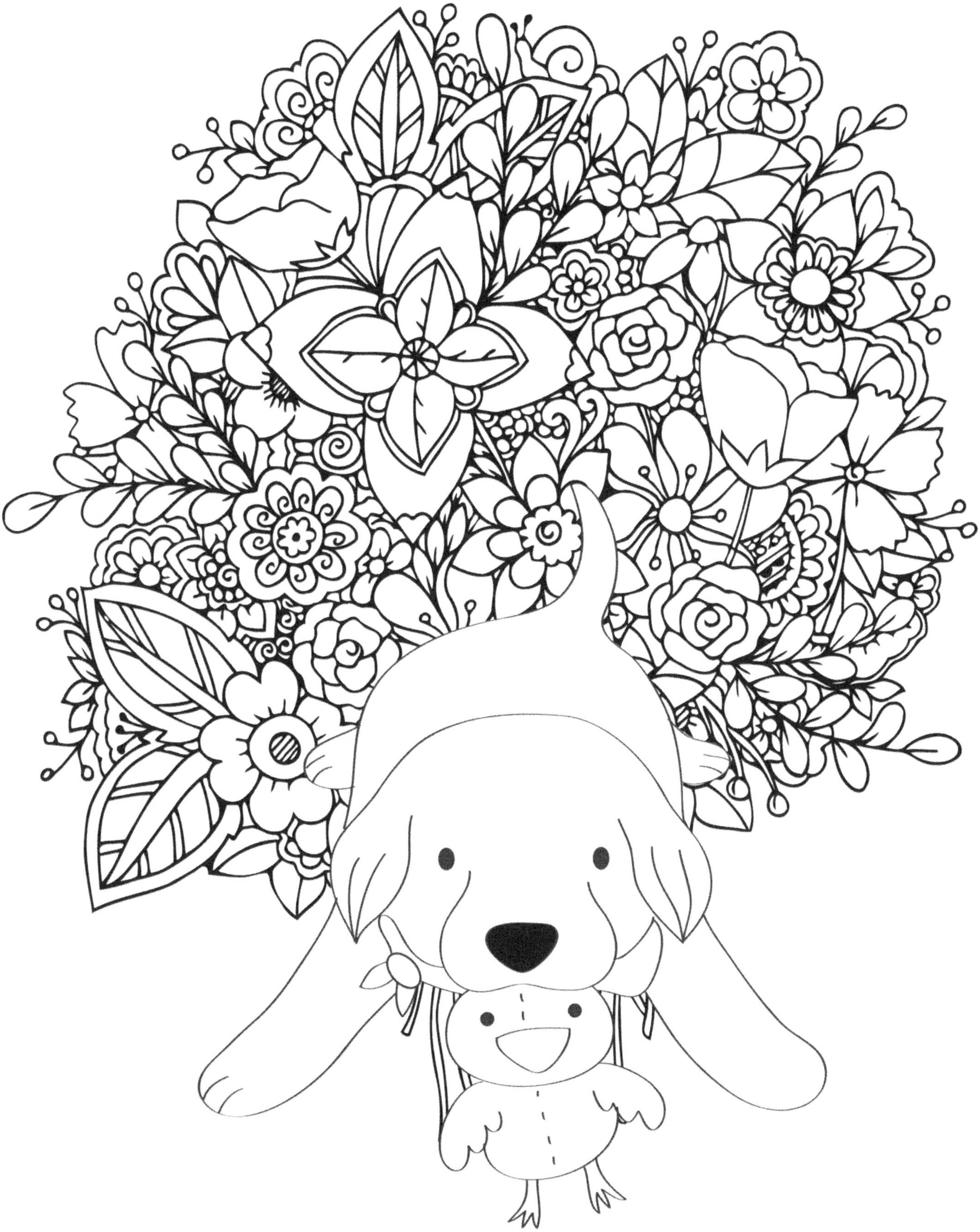

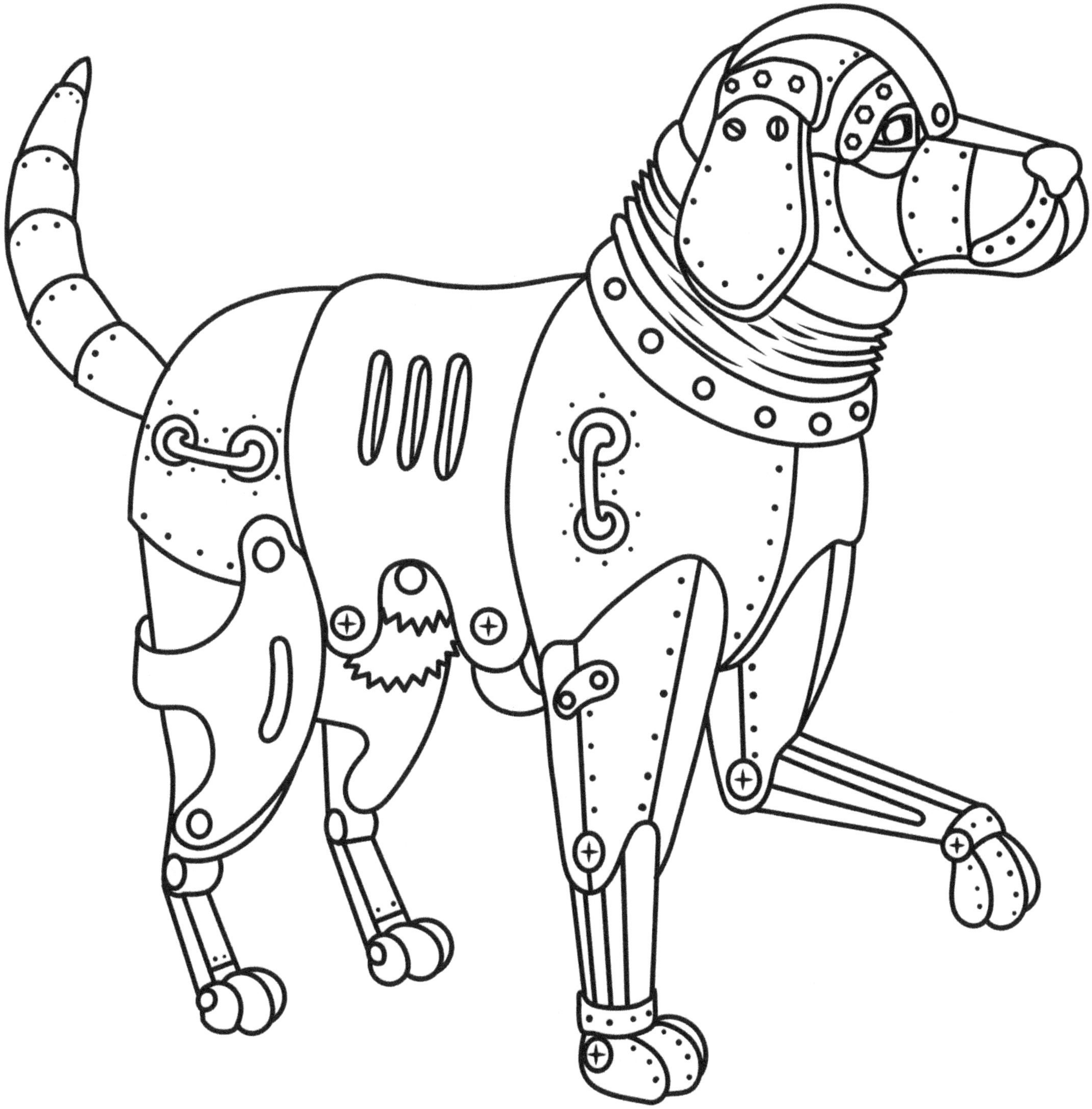

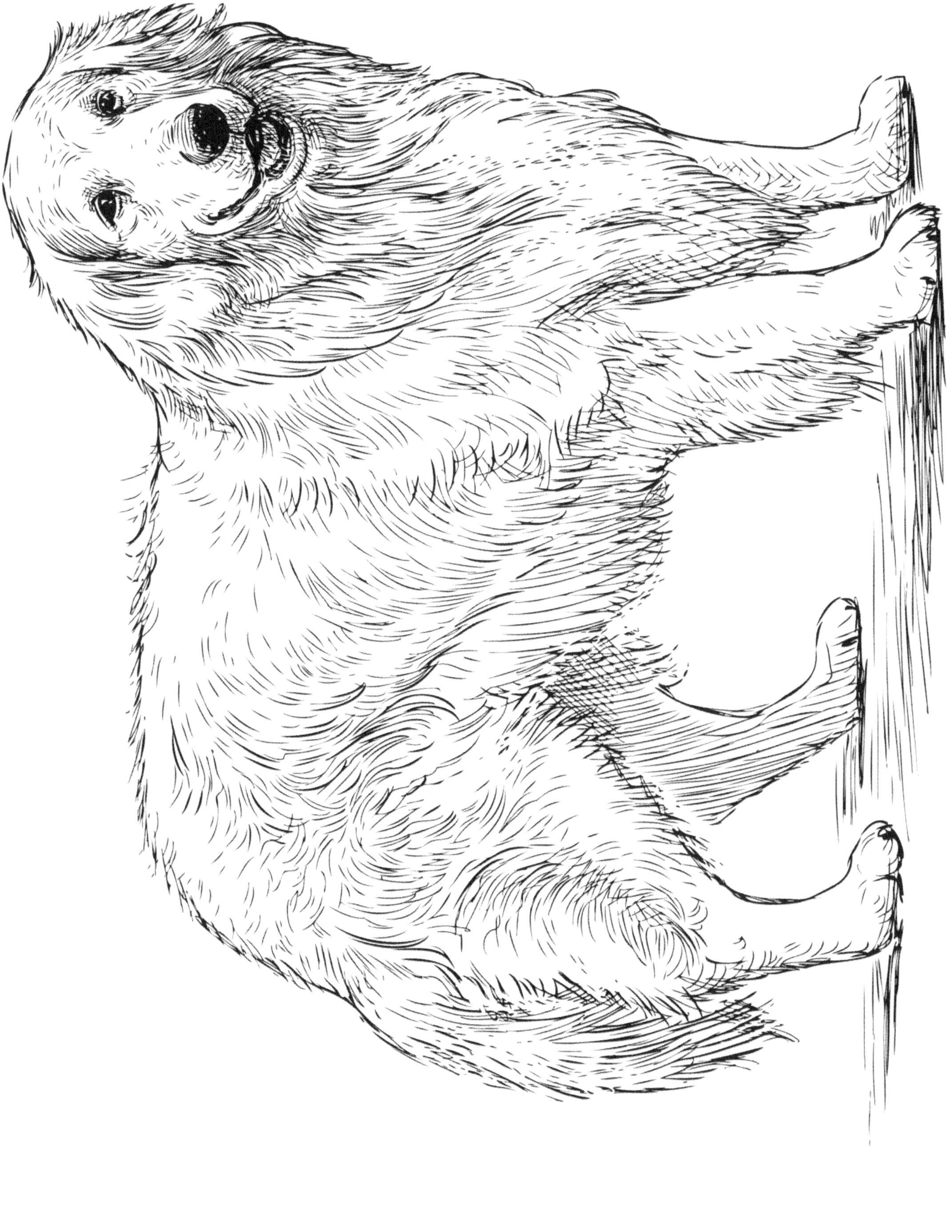

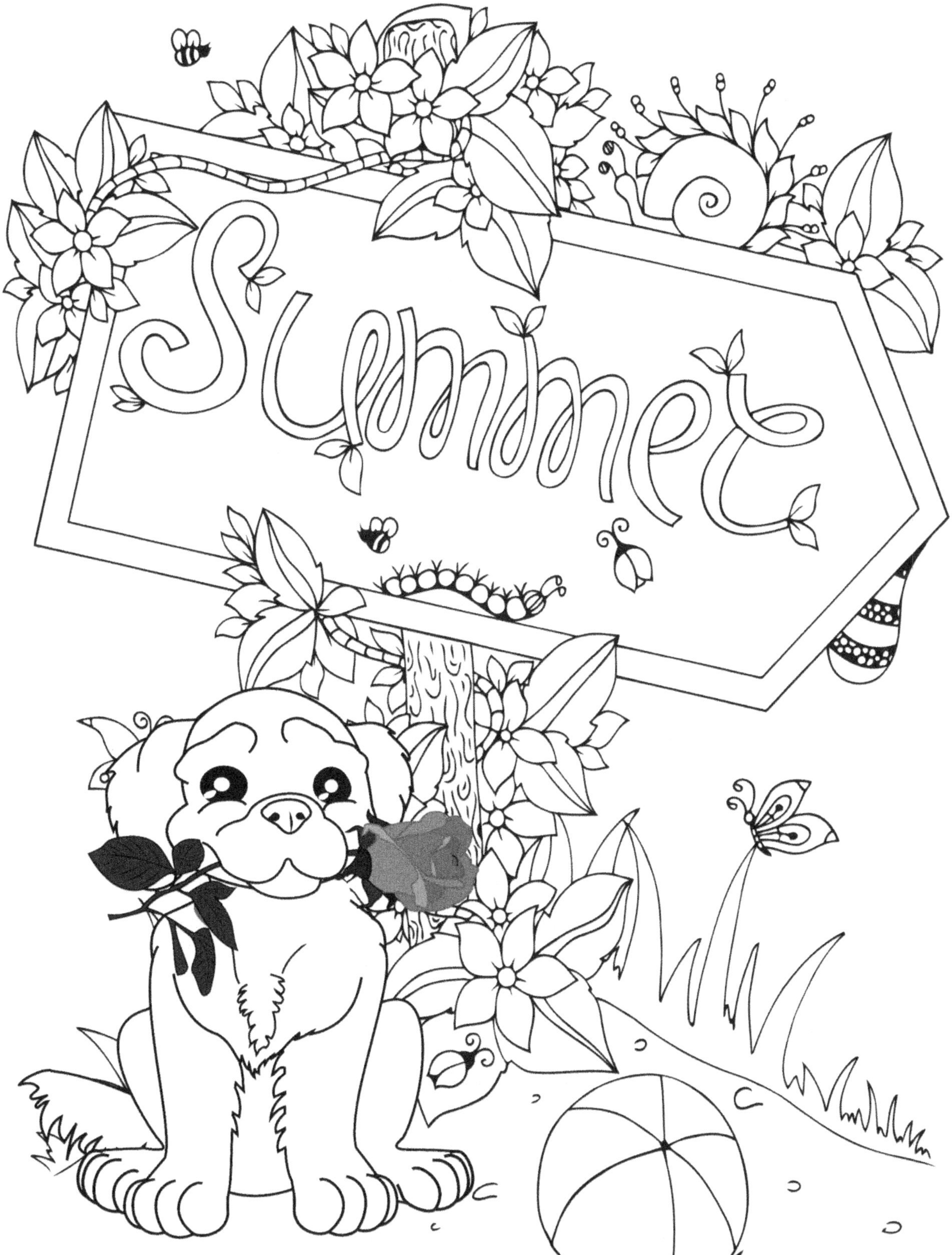
Summer

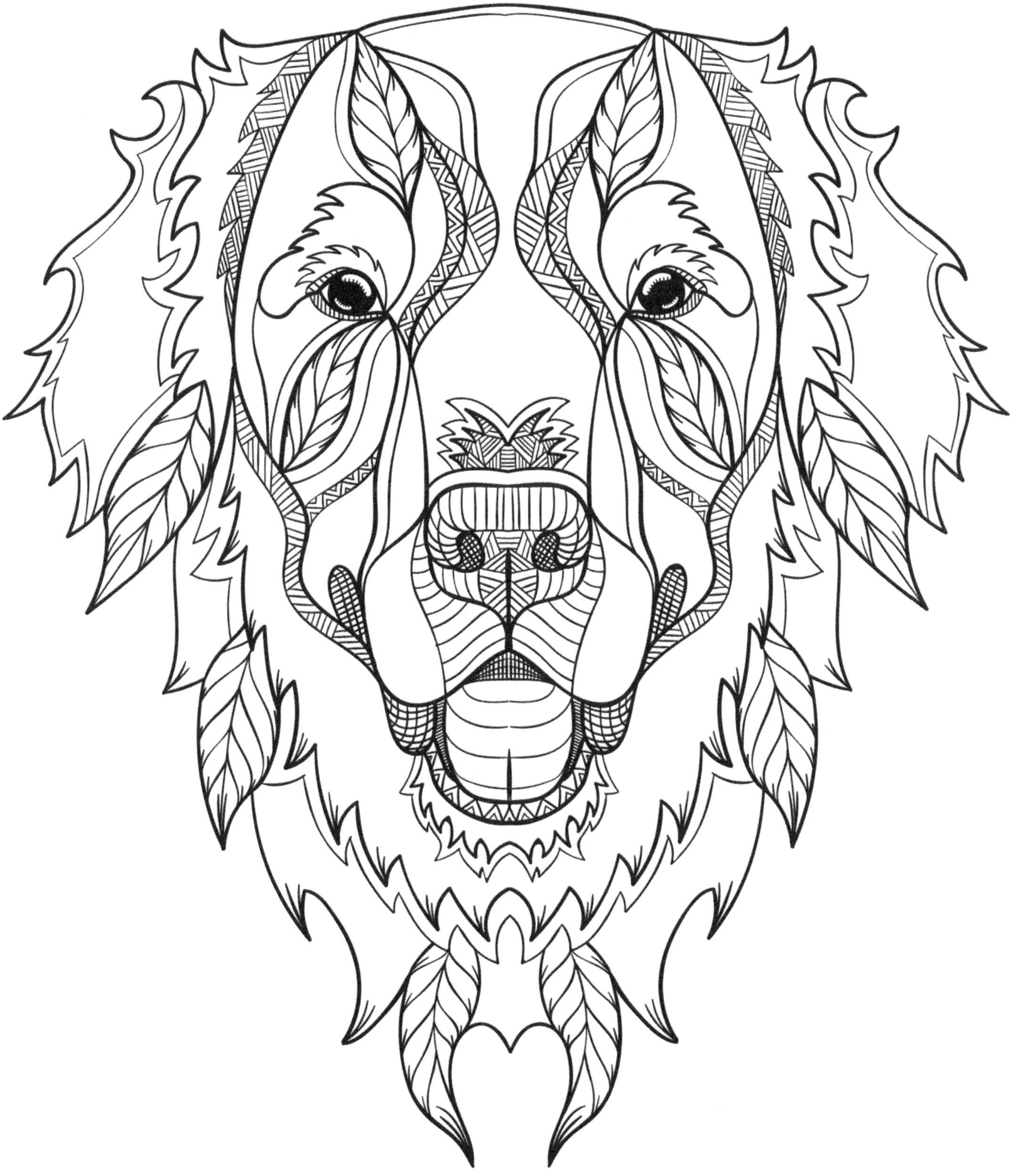

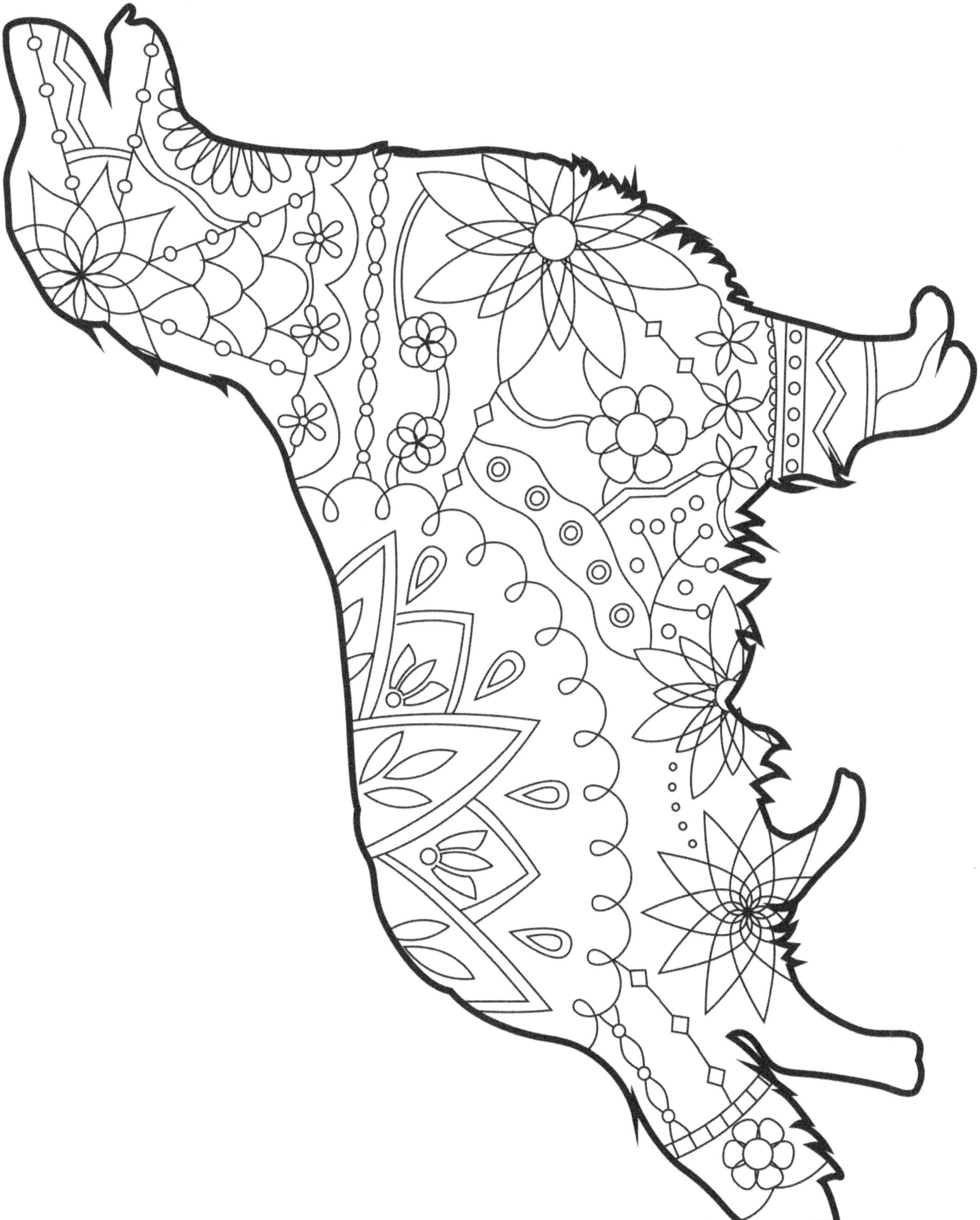

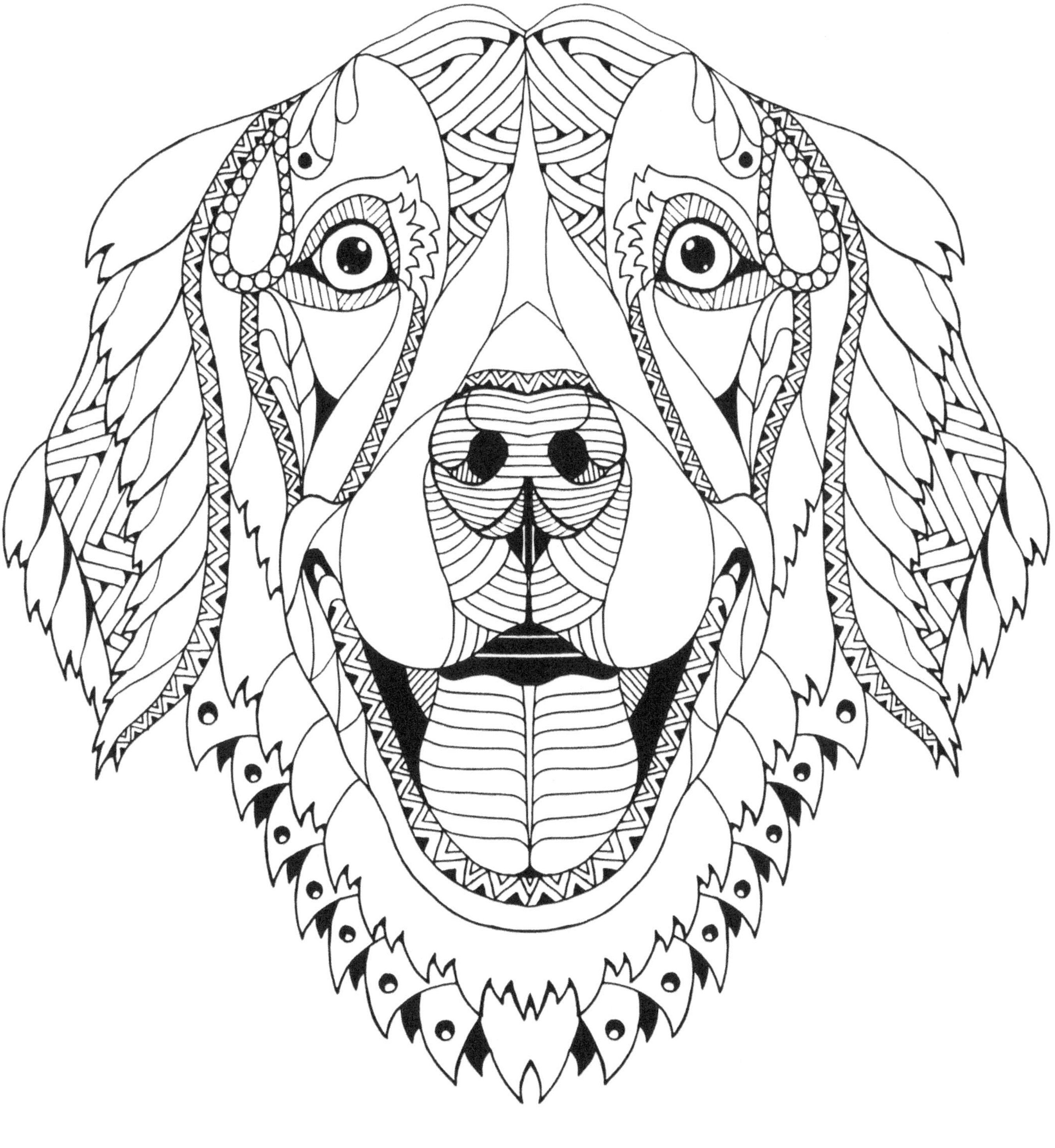

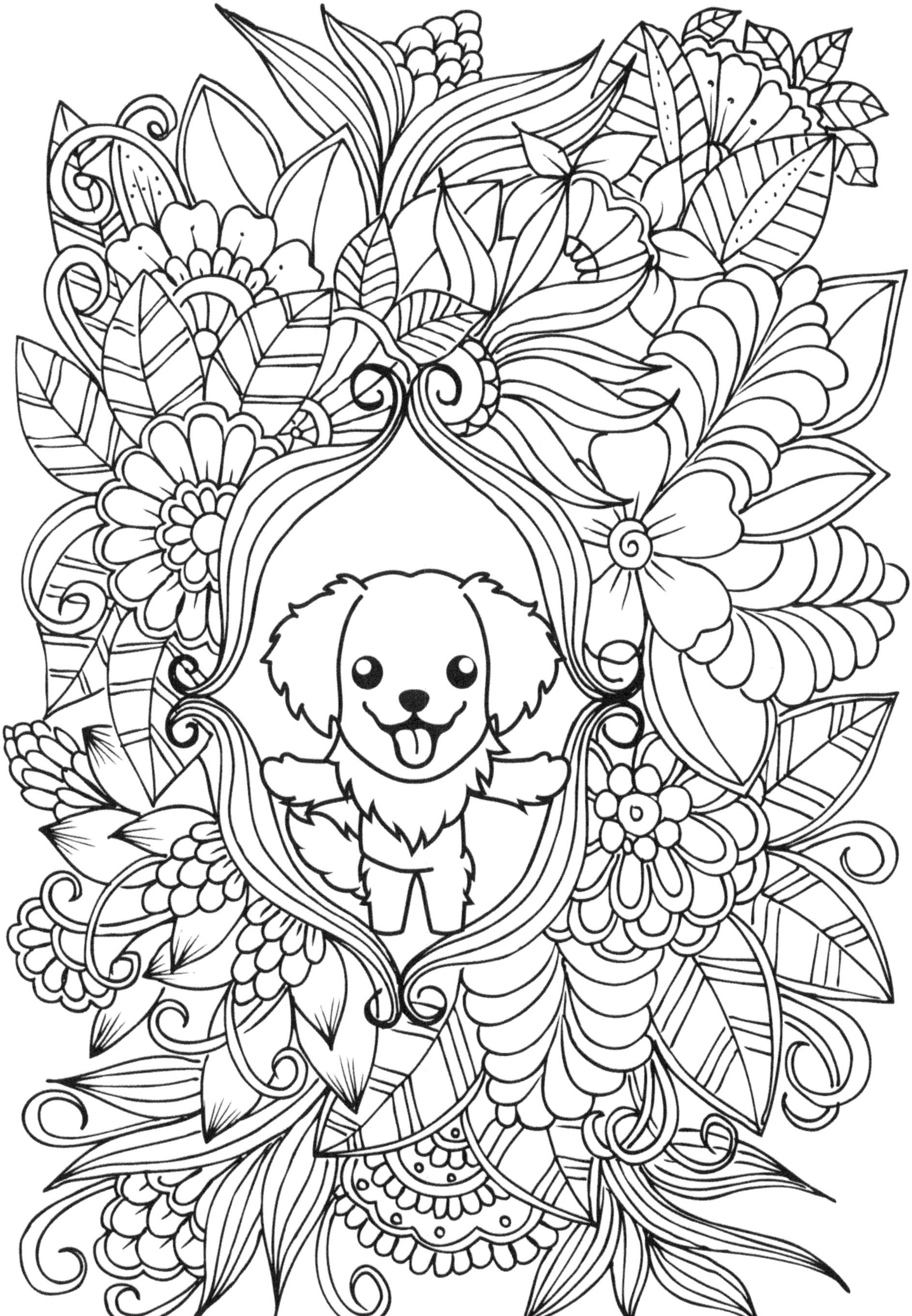

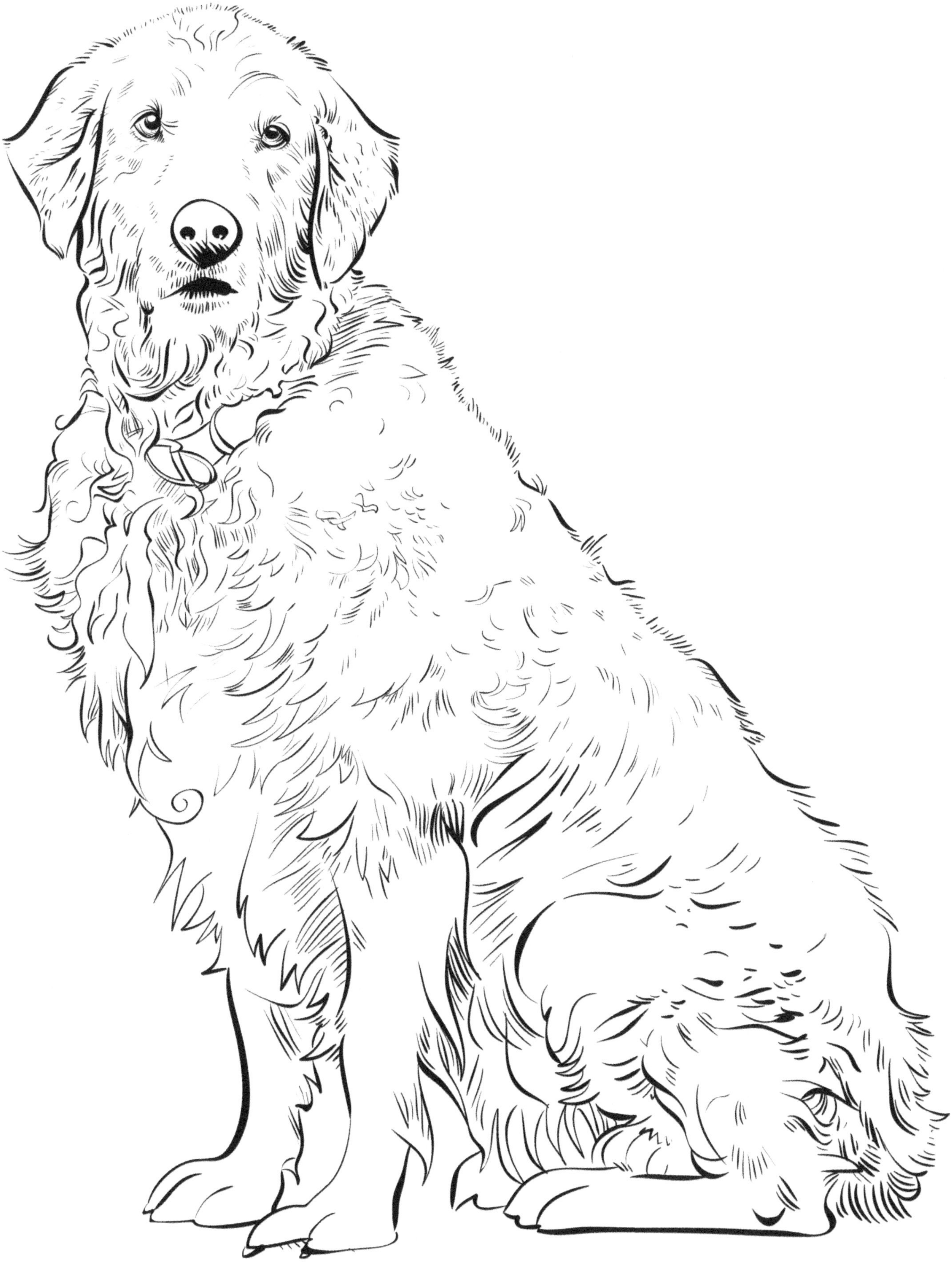

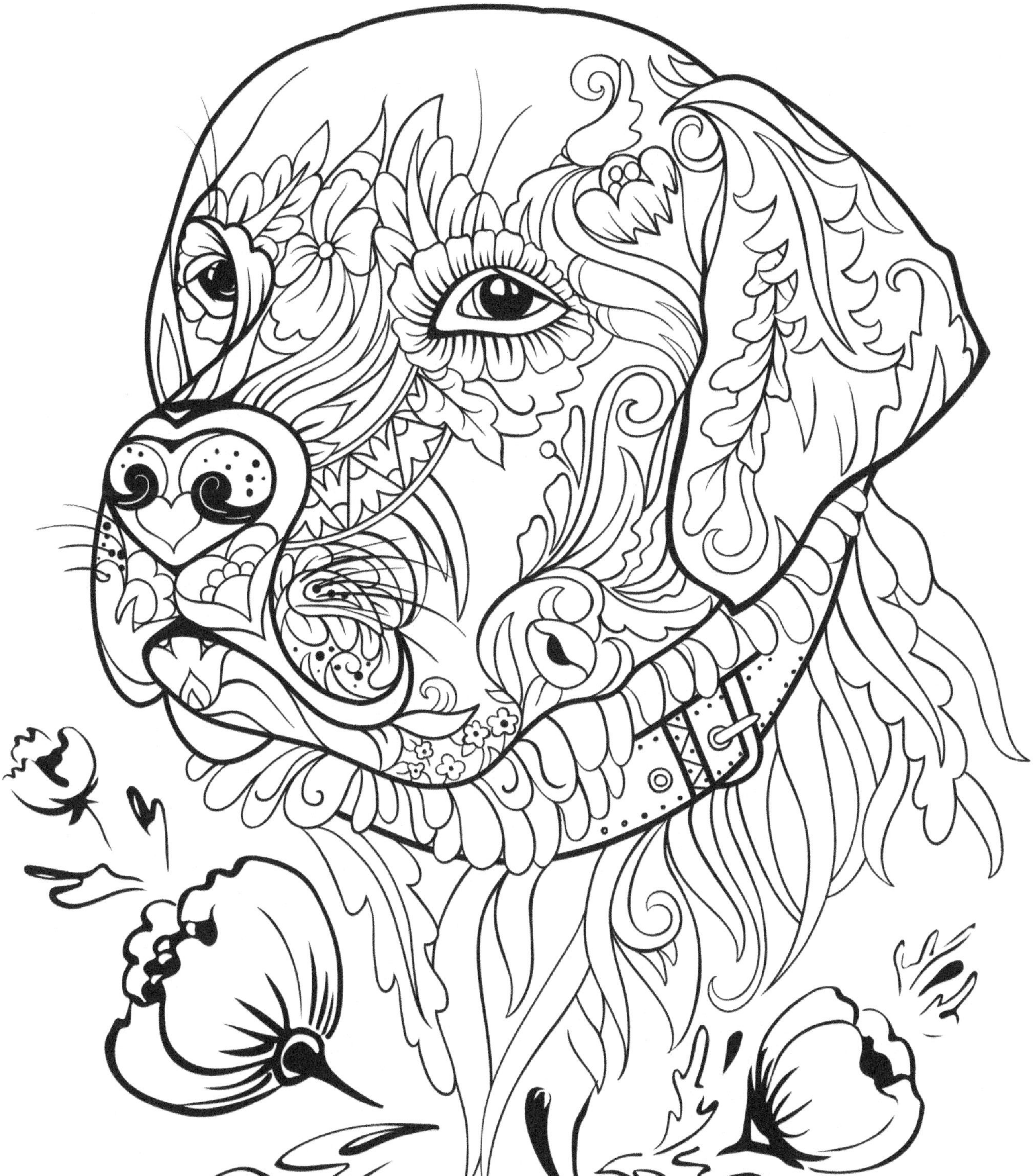

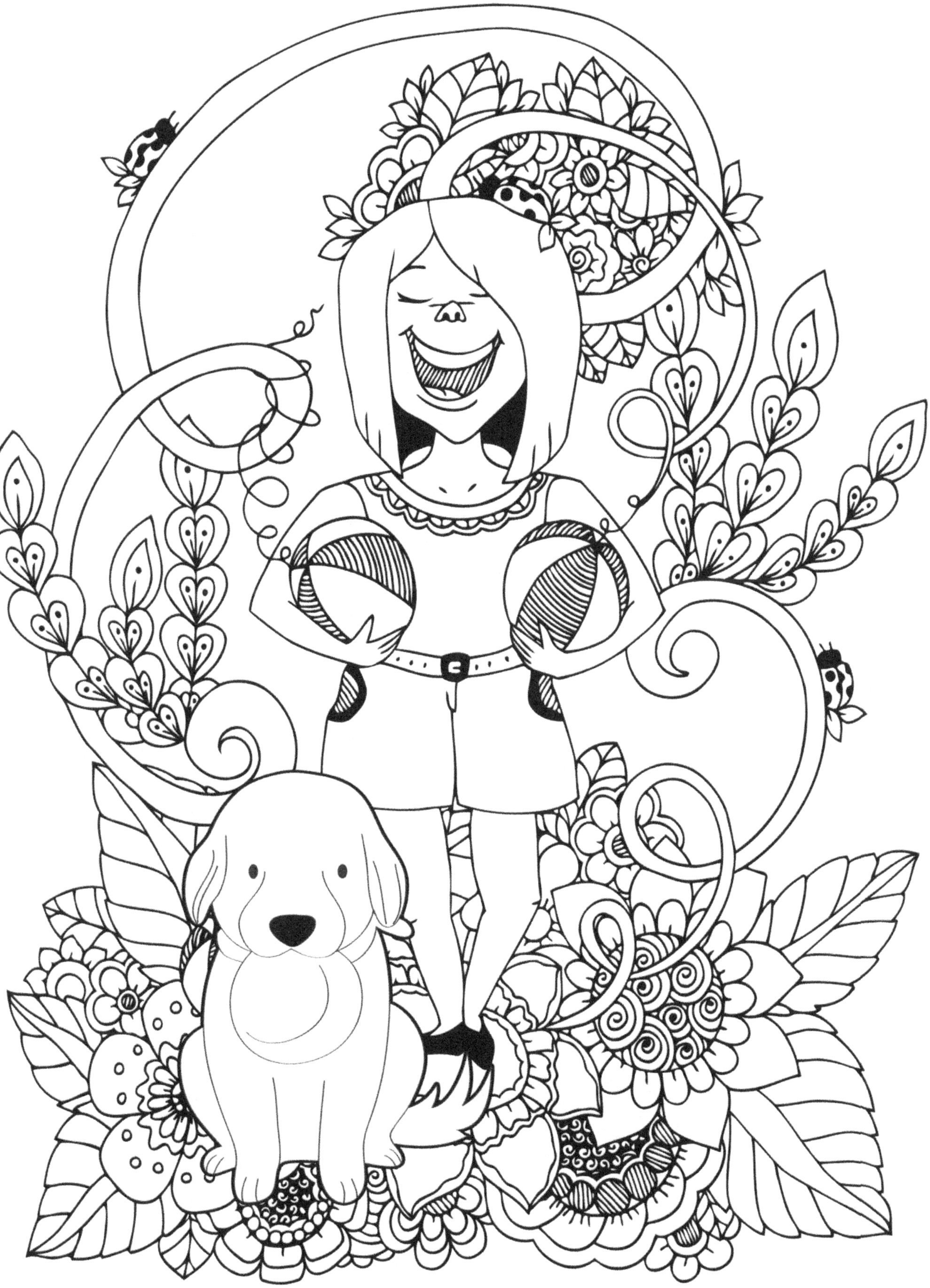

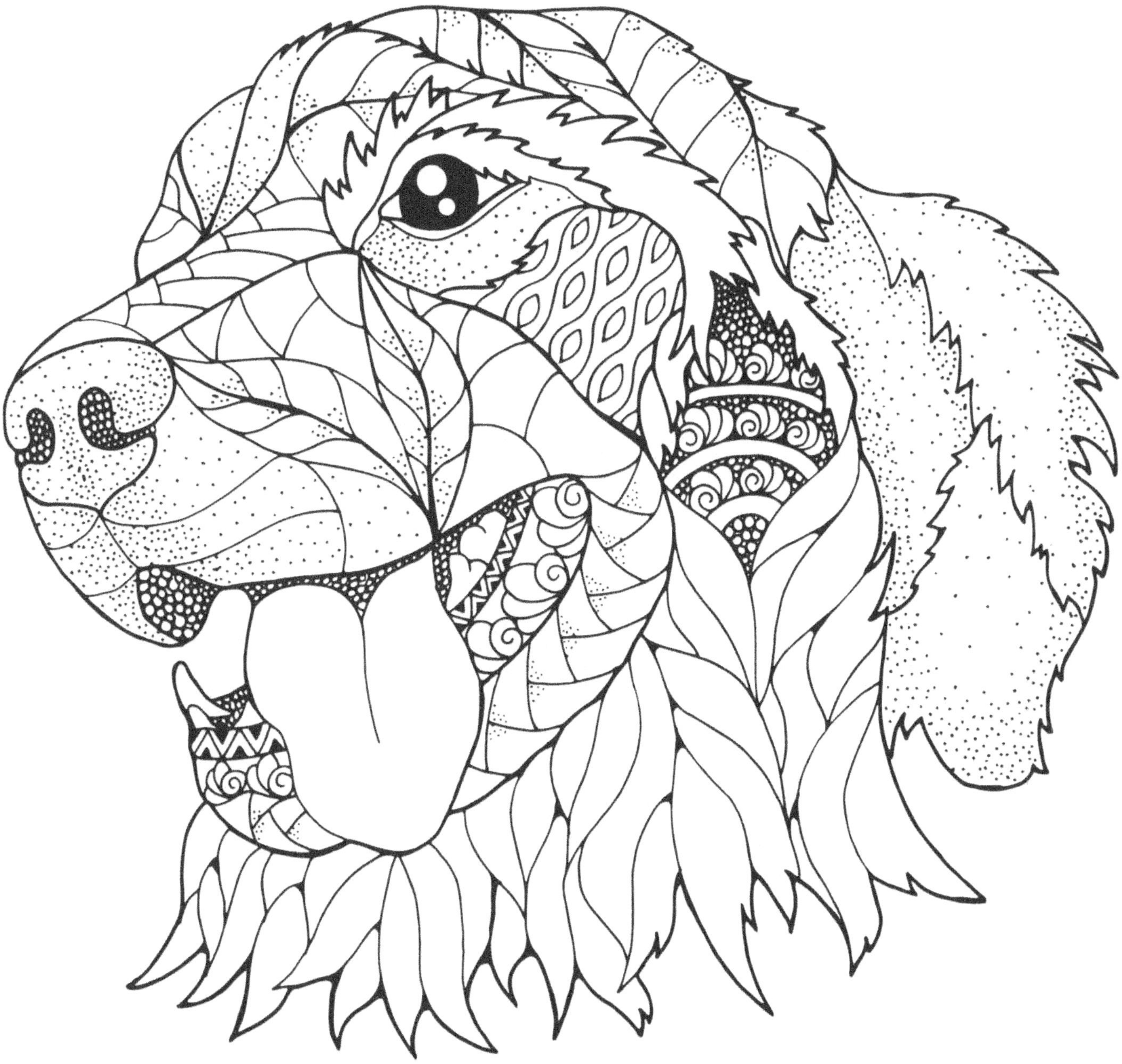

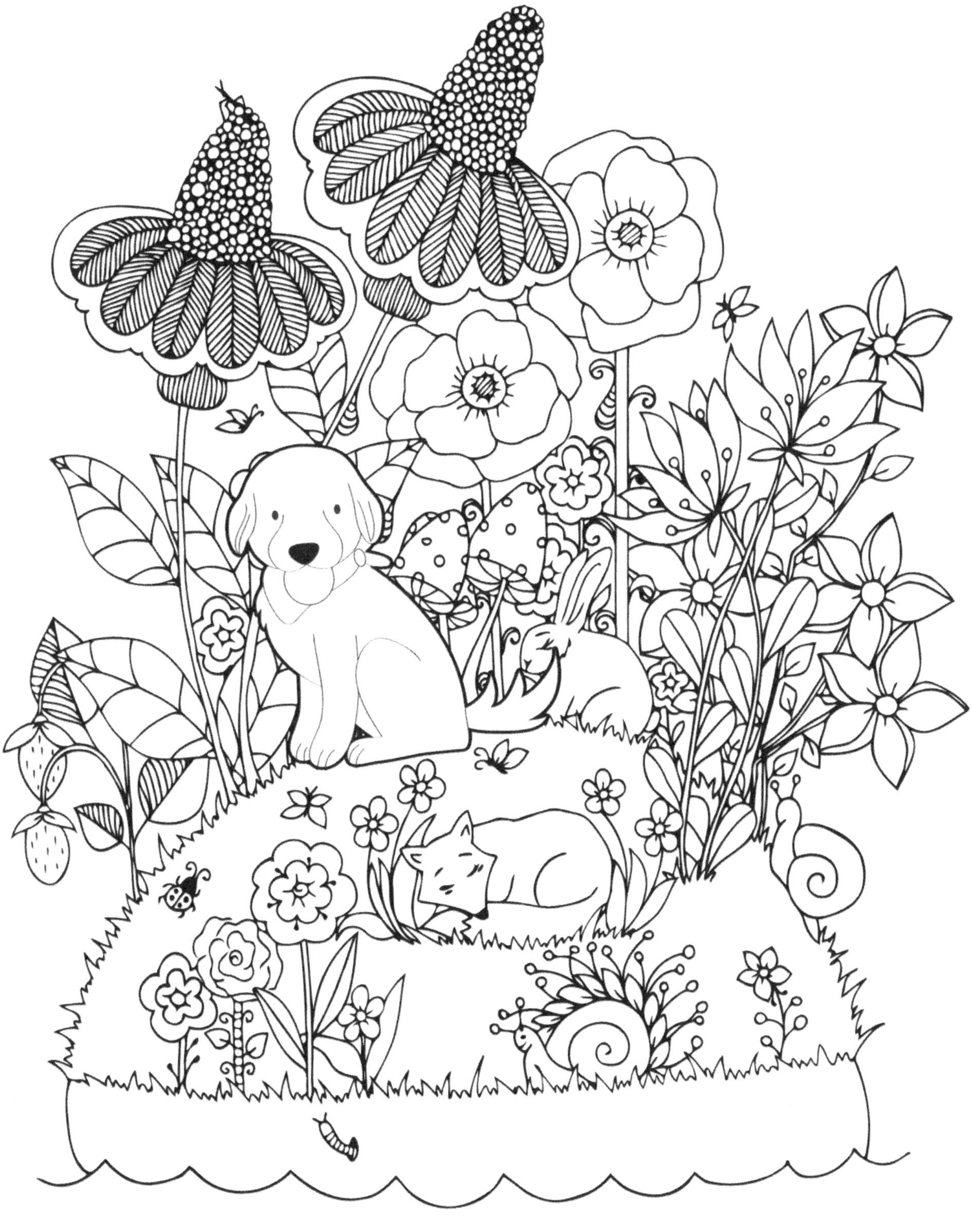

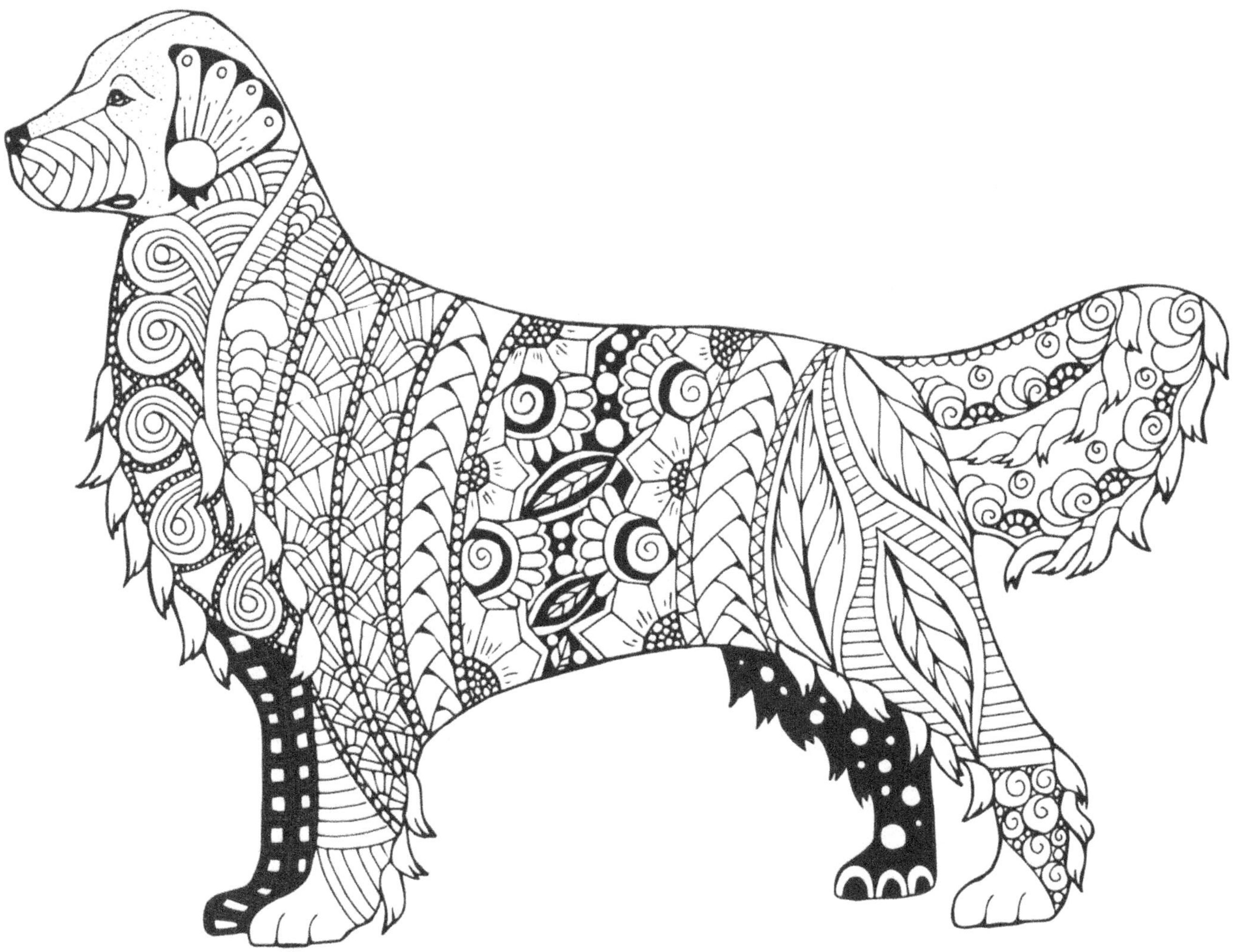

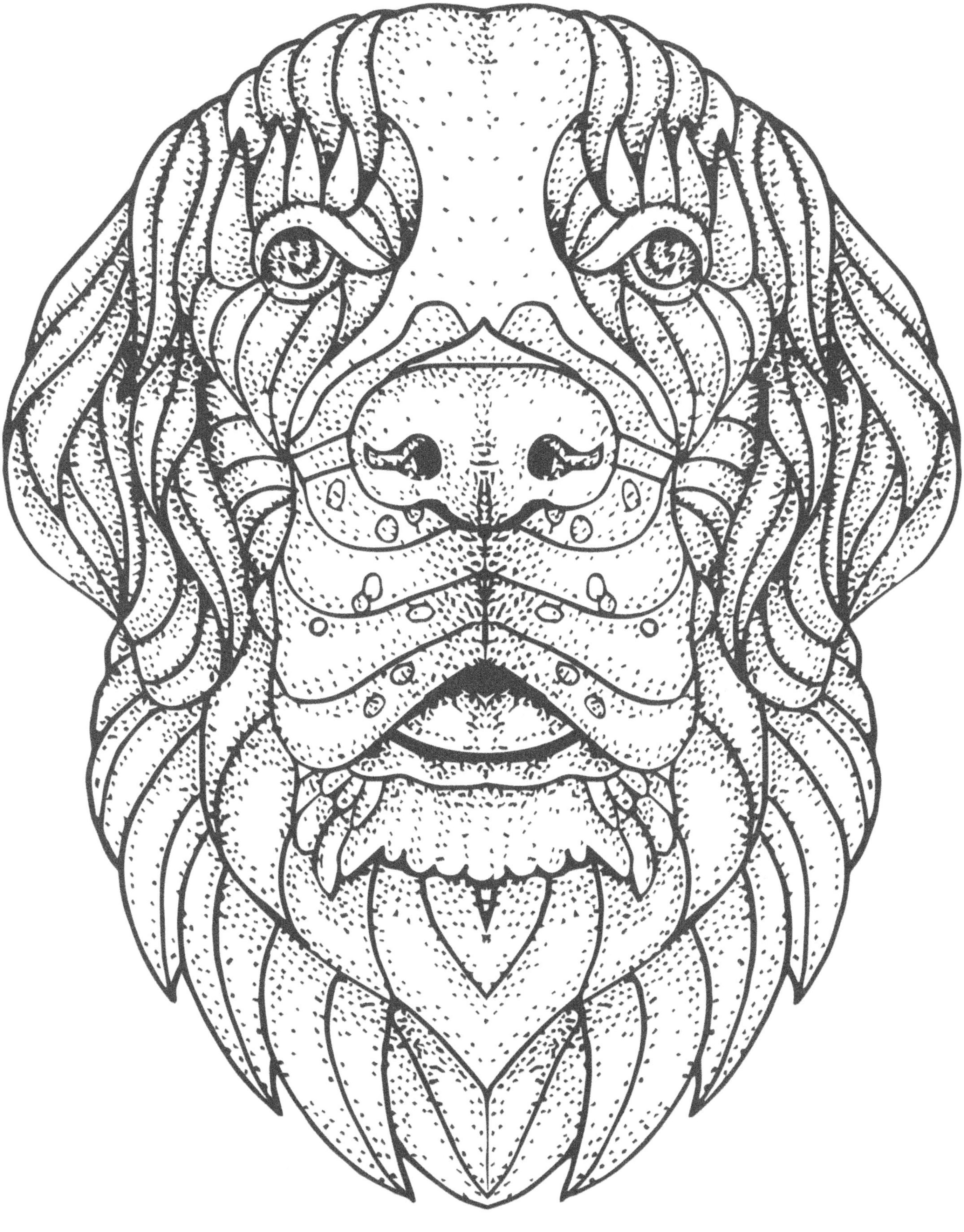

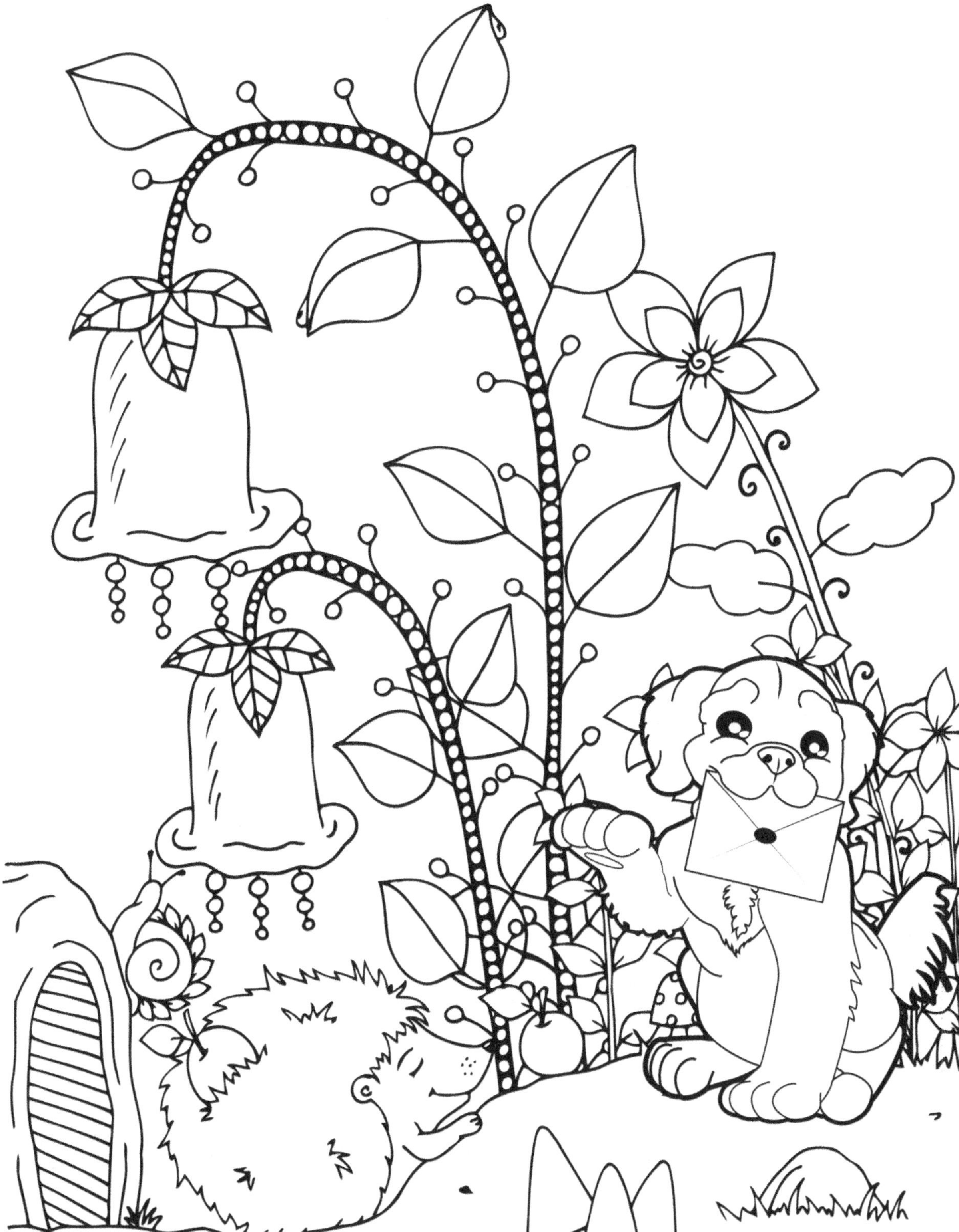

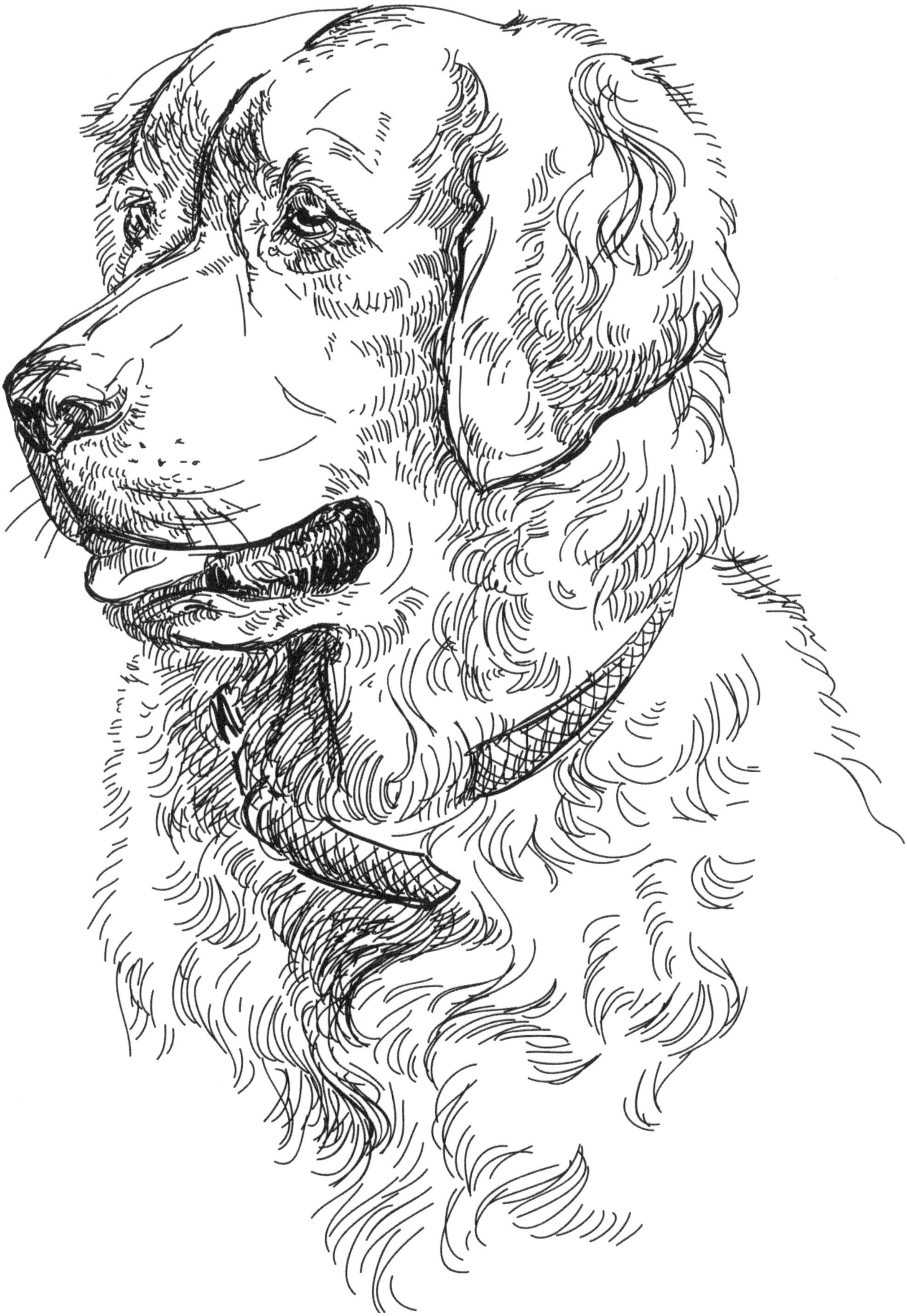

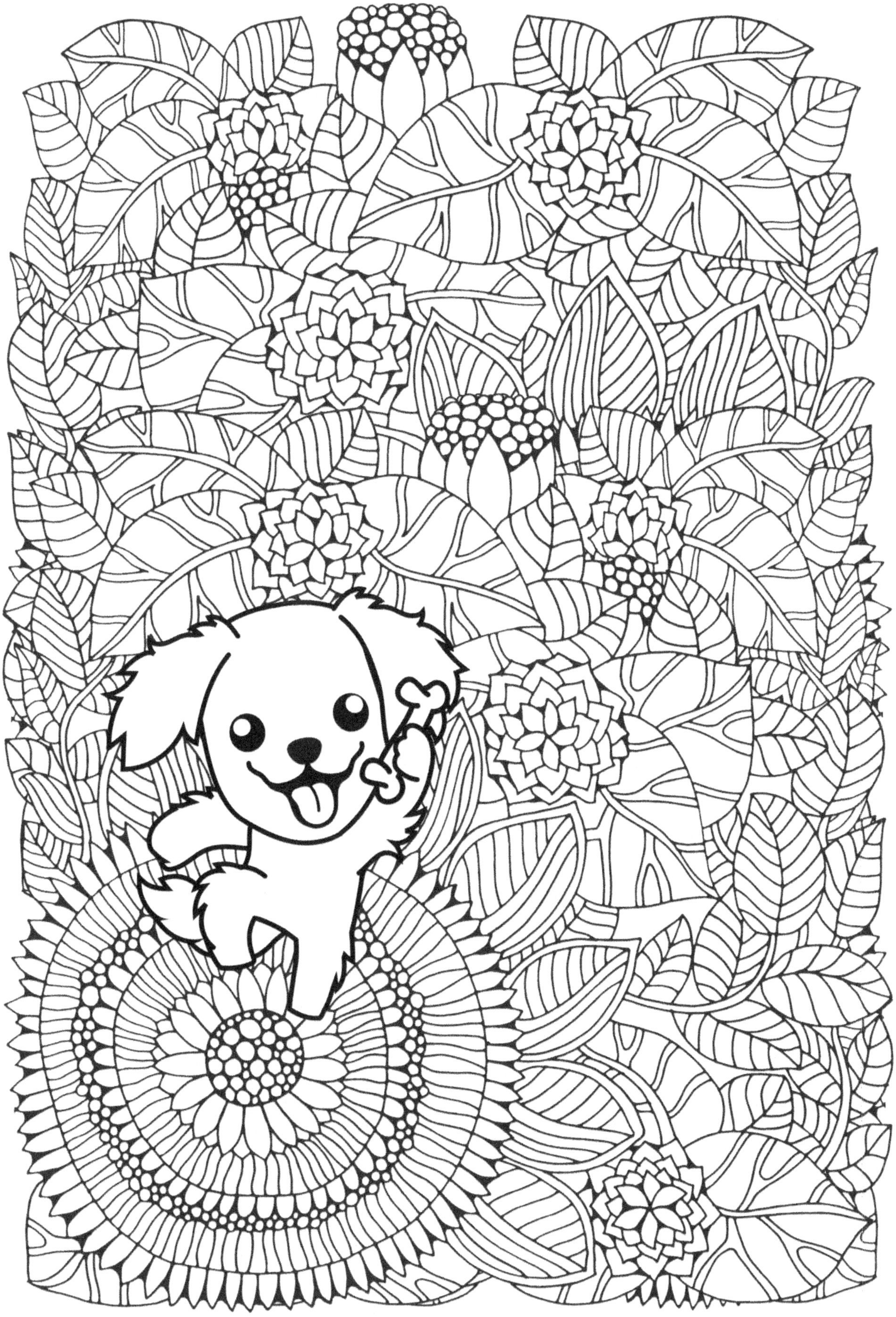

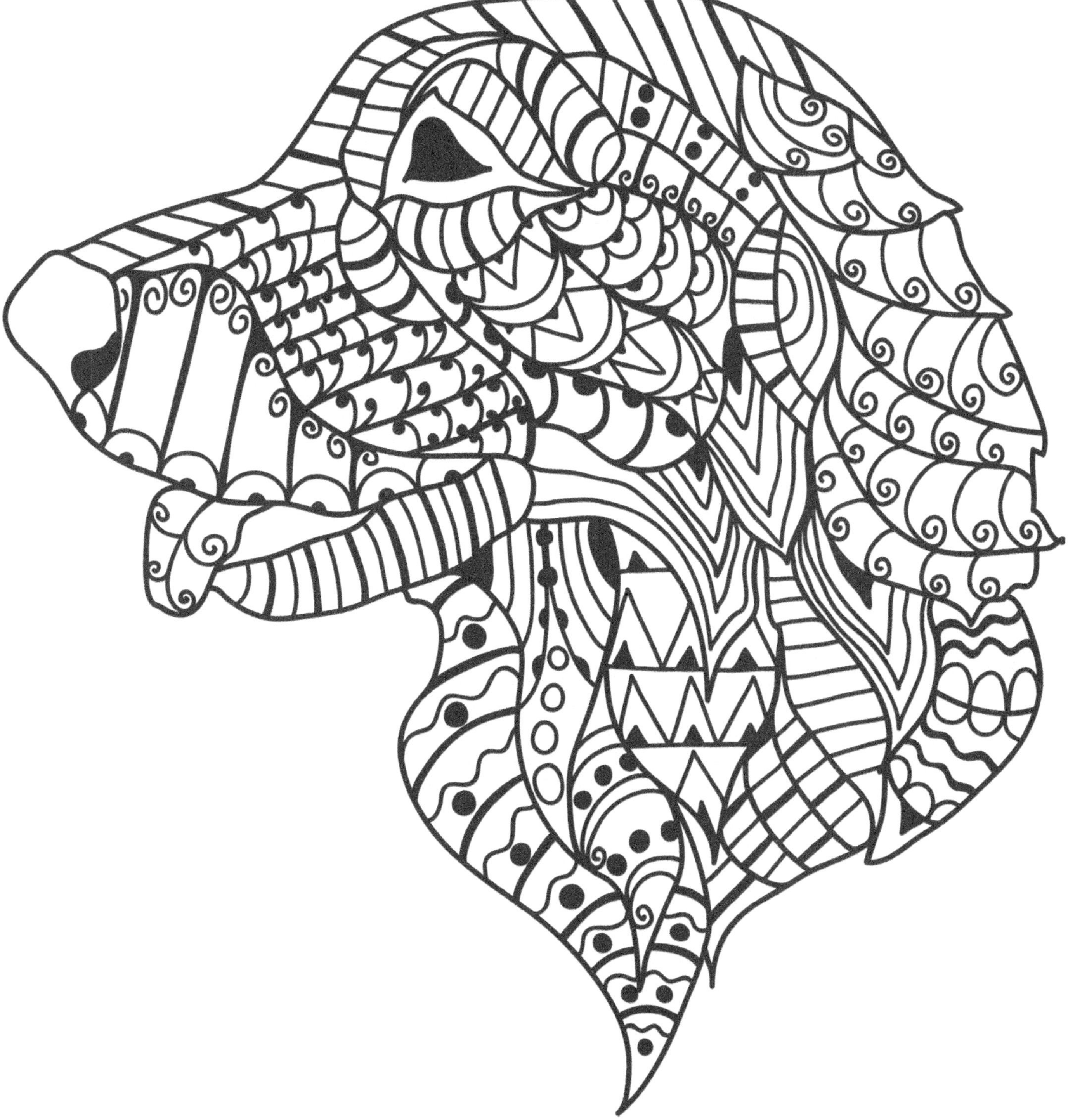

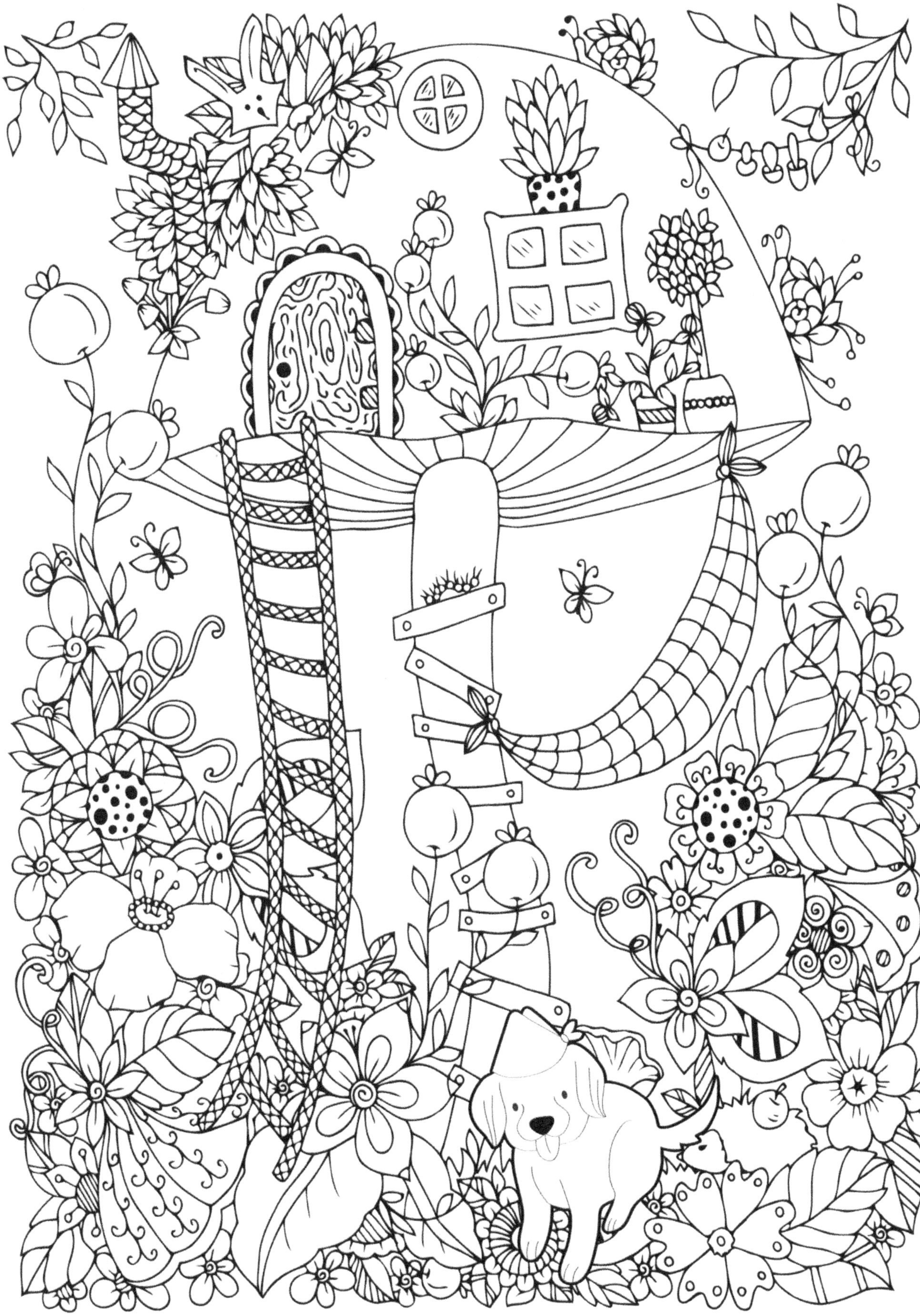

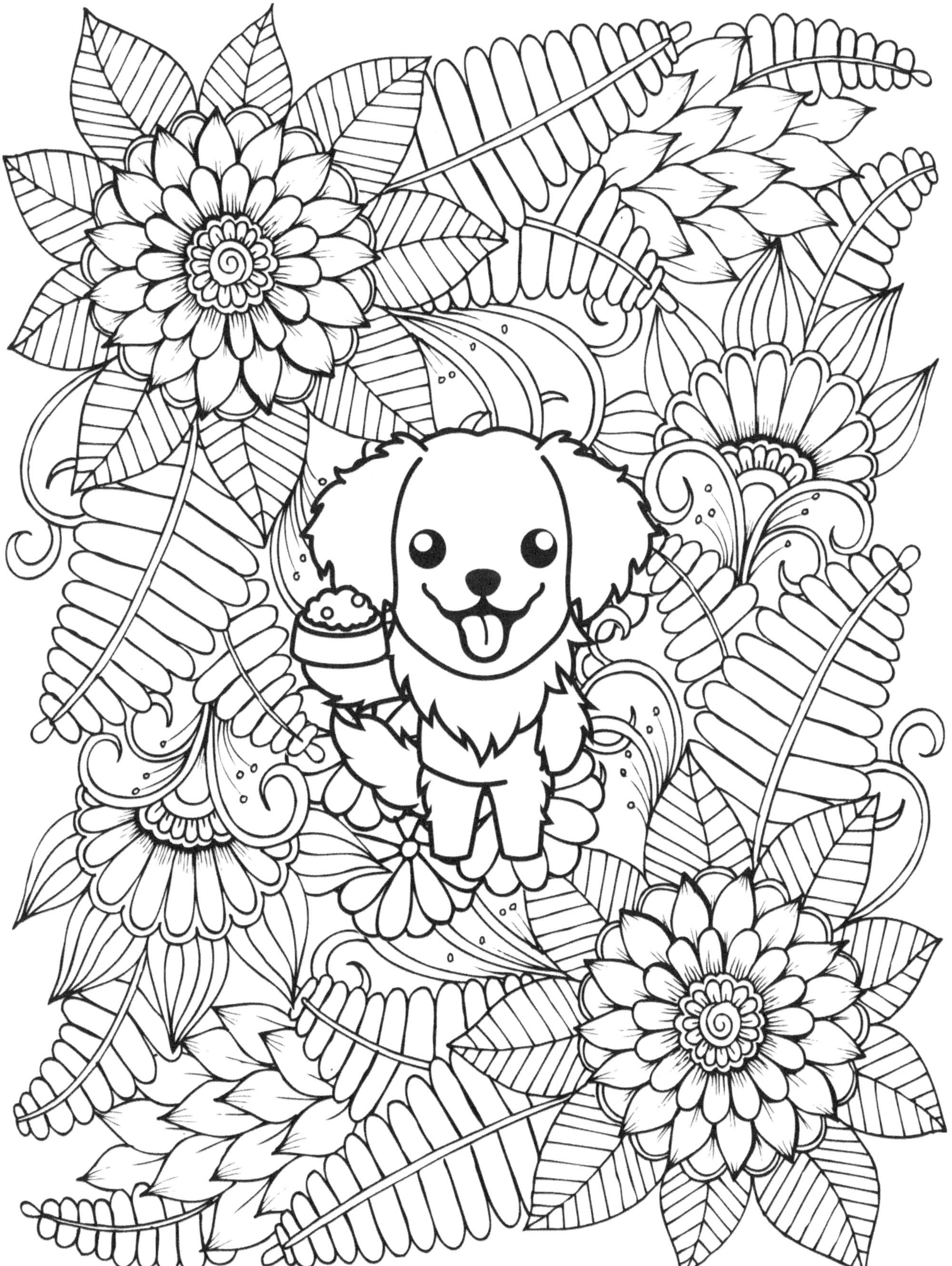

Made in the USA
Columbia, SC
02 August 2020

15362748R00057